THE JOURNEY WITHIN

A Spiritual Path to Recovery

Ruth Fishel

Illustrations by Bonny Lowell

Health Communications, Inc.
Deerfield Beach, Florida

Ruth Fishel
Serenity Inc.
Natick, Massachusetts 01760

Publishers: Peter Vegso
Gary Seidler
Editor: Marie Stilkind
Art Director: Reta Kaufman
Typographer: Kim Zaborski
Layout Artist: Dawn Bruce

Library of Congress Cataloging-in-Publication Data

Fishel, Ruth, 1935-
The journey within.

Bibliography: p.
1. Spiritual life. I. Title.
BL624.F53 1987   158'.1   87-180
ISBN 0-932194-41-9

Published by Health Communications, Inc.
Enterprise Center
3201 SW 15th Street
Deerfield Beach, FL 33442

Acknowledgments

I am deeply grateful to everyone who has written, taped, taught or researched on the subjects in this book before me. From the first book I read on meditation, a path seemed to clear before my very eyes and I was led from one book to another, from one course and workshop to another, and from one person to another. I knew from page one that I would write this book to serve as a tool to help people in growth and recovery. I have tried to acknowledge all ideas, sources and quotes used, but if I have missed someone, please forgive me and know that the error can be corrected in another printing.

My special thanks go to Sandy Bierig, for all her support, and for so very patiently and willingly editing my many early drafts that helped bring this book to an acceptable state with Health Communications:

. . . to Marie Stilkind, my editor, for all her encouragement, enthusiasm and good suggestions.

. . . to Bonny Lowell for all her wonderful artistic interpretations of my words and thoughts that bring a smile to so many pages;

. . . to Larry Rosenberg, my meditation teacher, and founder and teacher at Cambridge Insight Meditation Society. I thank him first for his gentle, sensitive and knowledgeable guidance and instructions and second for encouraging me to teach my first group at MCI-Framingham;

. . . all the women at Serenity House, in the SPRING program at Massachusetts Correctional Institute for Women, everyone on the staff at Serenity, Inc., and everyone who has come to my meditation classes. I developed a program that I believed would be helpful in recovery and through your daring to try it and then sharing yourselves and your experiences at a very deep and honest level, you have been an inspiration for me to write this book so that this program can be a help to all people who wish to grow.

Dedication

I dedicate this book with love to my three children, Debbie, Bob and Judy. Their own Spiritual Path to Recovery has been laden with many sharp turns and rough and rocky sections, but they have not stopped or turned back nor have they ever stopped supporting me on mine.

Dear Gentle Reader,

During the last five years of my drinking, I used to try to not drink on a daily basis. And yet everyday at around 3:30 as I was leaving work, all determination and resolutions would dissolve and my car, as if it had a mind of its own, would seem to be pulled almost magnetically to the package store. Alcohol was then to me a compulsion, an addiction, an obsession and, as I was only later to find out, a disease. In those days I did not know how not to drink.

Lately, that has been how this book has felt to me: a compulsion without the disease. I have not known how *not* to write this book! It has pulled at me, first gently and then with greater and greater urgency. This time I know I am being led to write it, that there really is a magnetic power, that a Power Greater Than Myself is leading me and I cannot *not* write it!

There are many good books out about meditation. I read at least 40 or 50 of them for background for this book and for my own meditation practice. There are certainly wonderful, God-given programs like Alcoholics Anonymous, Narcotics Anonymous, Gamblers Anonymous, Overeaters Anonymous, etc. to help with your addictions. There are also Adult Children of Alcoholics, Al-Anon, Alateen, Emotions Anonymous, just to name a few. And there are good courses out there by excellent meditation teachers.

So why has this book become so important to me?

As a recovering alcoholic, an adult child of an alcoholic and a person who never dared to live in truth and love for many years, I have been transformed by the work that I have been doing and I want to share it with you, my reader. I am 51 years old and I drank for 21 of those years, 14 of those years daily. I have been sober 13 years, as of this writing, and seven of them have been spent in different forms of meditation. Thirty-seven of them were spent trying to be someone I was not, but thought I should be.

If you are currently struggling with any of the issues I have mentioned, I hope you will find some answers by taking some simple steps. Whatever your addiction (drugs, work, sex, overeating), you can still live life to its fullest.

The writing of this book has been an extraordinary growth experience for me. As I have gathered together my material and experiences and written about it, I knew that I had to be absolutely honest with you, dear reader, as well as with myself. I realized that as I was sharing in this book, I was at no point judging myself or was ashamed of who I am or have been. My only fear was that if I tell you who I am, you won't like me. That fear I have found to be from old tapes, from other times, and has nothing to do with the reality of today. This book has helped me work that through. I am almost grateful for that!

May this book make as much of a difference in your life as it has made in mine. And may you give to others what has been given to you, so that those still hurting and in the dark will be able to see their Higher Power and get in touch with the energies for Good and for Love and for God in the universe.

The combinations that I have found that worked for me can work for you. Please know that the lessons in this book *will work* for you. If you will only act as if you have the faith to get well, then all the powers and the energies of the universe will shine a light so bright upon your path that you will be magnetically led to a transformation of happiness and self-fulfillment so great it will amaze you. And this is not an exaggerated promise. I know because I have lived it!

With Love and Faith,

Ruth Fishel

CONTENTS

1

Now is the Time

"Someday, after we have mastered the winds, the waves, the tides and gravity, we shall harness for God the energies of love. Then, for the second time in the history of the world, man will have discovered fire."

Teilhard de Chardin

I believe that deep within every human being lies the true essence of our being, a spark of life and love, a pure spark of energy that gives us all our sameness. Each experience thereafter establishes our uniqueness.

Each moment and experience of life after birth either kindles or covers this spark. But no matter what we experience even if we can no longer feel this spark, no matter how many layers and layers of negative experiences have covered and buried our spark of life, it can never be completely extinguished.

Love, kindness, caring, touching and gentleness nurture and stoke this spark into a warm and constant glow. Those of us who have had the good fortune to be brought up in such an atmosphere are truly lucky human beings. Some have been fortunate enough to have been born to two normal, loving, intelligent, financially secure parents. These parents loved and gave their children discipline and encouragement. Their children were held and touched and felt love and they learned to give love back. They were taught to be independent, self-sufficient and highly motivated. They were taught about morals and standards and that life was about love. Growing up under these loving circumstances stoked that tiny spark. These children grew up to be trusting people, capable of giving and receiving love naturally and easily.

And for the rest of us, I write this book!

The rest of us were also born with this tiny spark of love and life. And to oversimplify *our* upbringing just to make a point, the alternatives to the ideal upbringing were . . .

1. deprivation of love
   or
2. inconsistent conditional love
   or
3. gray areas between both.

Most of us fit into number 3.

When our parents came together, they were complete with their own individual sets of guilts, fears, hangups, dependencies and addictions. Mix them together and not only do you have a parent A and parent B to deal with but you now have all the *stuff*, the chemistry, the interaction of the ingredients of the two packages, that make a whole new entity: package C.

To confuse the issue even more, maybe you don't always have a Mom, or the same Mother all the time or a Dad or the same Dad all the time. Maybe there are other "Moms" or "Dads" entering or leaving the scene. Maybe alcohol and/ or other drugs are around. Hard financial times and other siblings enter the picture. There is suddenly someone new to share all these goings on with, and more chemistry and energy is added!

And we could go on to list hundreds of other possible combinations, i.e., finances, the quality of education, ethnic background and religion, and so on. All leading to one large result . . . lack of self-esteem, self-hatred, self-loathing or anger directed outward towards other people, places and things.

For most of us our spark doesn't always get nurtured to its fullest capacity. Most of us have so much negative stuff that gets poured into us and on top of us that we no longer know that we have this spark of life.

Whatever we felt, whatever we wanted, who we became for a long time was the result of what went on from the active, energetic interchange of situations and personalities throughout our lives.

We took all of it in, absorbed the ingredients, and at some point made certain decisions, such as . . .

"I will never act like my mother or father!"

    or

"If I could only get married and get out of this mess, my life would be better!"

    or

"If I am good, maybe Daddy will come back."

    or

"Just one more drink (or pill or drug or chocolate) and I will feel better (or work better or study harder)"

    or a sudden discovery, such as . . .

"When I am sick, she really pays attention to me!"

These are just a few examples of the conscious decisions that some of us make to give us hope so that we can dream of escape from unpleasant situations.

All these decisions to do or not do something again were planned so that we would either feel better in the future or feel better now by depending on something or someone other than ourselves (i.e., pills, booze, relationships). And we kept on doing these same things over and over again, waiting for things to get better!

I remember as if it were yesterday an afternoon when I was around five years old. My mother was having some of her friends over for mah-jongg. A few women had already arrived and were sitting with my mother in the living room waiting for the others. My new baby brother, the intruder in my life and the thief of the attention that once was only for me, was being held by one of my mother's friends.

I can see myself skipping across the room and climbing up and sitting on my mother's lap. I can hear myself whispering shyly to her, "I haven't sat on your lap for a long, long time."

Her response was, "My, you have a bony tush!"

I remember getting slowly off her lap without moving a muscle in my face, without changing my expression. I was sure that everyone had heard. I knew everyone knew my shame. I clearly remember deciding that I would never get on her lap again.

Did my "non-touching nature" begin then? Did this shamefully horrible feeling get buried in my subconscious so that it took me 33 more years before I could feel comfortable enough to spontaneously hug someone? Another child might have responded totally differently. A child who was not as supersensitive might have just laughed and thought she was joking. Maybe she was! But I knew for me that I would never take another chance to feel so bad in front of anyone ever again.

I grew up believing that I was "not as good as . . .", "not as pretty as . . .", "not as smart as . . ." anyone my mother wanted me to be like. It was always (or so I remember it as *always*) "Why can't you play with dolls like Elyse?" I liked to play baseball with the boys! Or "Why can't you wear dresses like Margie?" I liked to wear dungarees and my father's old shirts and climb trees and dig holes.

My personal escape of choice, although I did not know it at the time, became alcohol. When I found alcohol, I finally thought I was as good as everyone else! It took alcohol to make me feel as pretty as the other girls! It took a few drinks to make me feel like other people. I always thought that everyone else was "normal", except me.

I always felt like the outsider, like I didn't fit. I was extraordinarily self-conscious and thought everyone was watching and criticizing every move I made, every word I uttered, even every expression on my face. Looking back I see clearly that it didn't matter who I was with. Family, friends, acquaintances or strangers, everyone else (the big *They*) always fit into their neat, comfortable circle. I would always be the outsider. The only time that this was not so for me was when I was either playing sports, at summer camp, on my roof, or beside the wonderful, private pond I discovered where I could be alone and paint or write poetry. Only then could I lose my self-consciousness and be spontaneously myself.

When I discovered alcohol, I was finally good enough. When I had a few drinks, I felt "normal", too!

My belief for the next 20 years became, "If I have another drink, I will feel better."

And my life continued to get worse.

Insanity is repeating the same things over
and over again,
expecting different results.

2

Turning Stumbling Blocks Into Stepping Stones

"You are going to find a star to light your path."

A Course in Miracles

"We cannot leave the trap until we know that we are in it. We are in a needless imprisonment."

Marilyn Ferguson

Until I finally surrendered to the fact that I was an alcoholic and began, with the guide of the 12 steps to look within to heal and grow, I had absolutely no chance of ever getting better. I had spent my entire life playing the *"if"* game or the *"when"* game! "If only she would understand me . . ." or "If only we had more money . . .", or "When I finish college, it will be better". Always later. Always out there. Always someone else.

I think I bought (and read) every self-help book on the market; each time thinking, "Yes! This is *it*!" and indeed feeling better for a day or two. But then life always seemed to go on . . . business as usual. And I was miserable again and depressed again and slid into my "self-pity" role of "No matter what I do it doesn't matter" and "No one will ever understand me." "Poor me!"

Like Walking Into One Big Dark Room

Imagine that you are walking into a completely dark room. You keep bumping into things and bruising yourself.

You keep trying to do it differently . . . maybe walking in to the right or in to the left. You try one entrance after another and the same thing keeps on happening. More bruises and bangs and scars as you bang into tables and chairs. You can try this over and over again and achieve the same results.

Maybe you decide that if you walk in on a Tuesday, it will be different.

Or on a Friday afternoon.

Or with a friend on a Thursday morning.

Or . . . you can try a different approach. You can *change* your approach!

You Can Put A Light On!

You can put a light on each piece of furniture that you have been bumping into and you can . . .

**Move
The Furniture!**

Looking back, it feels as if I was living in that one big, dark, black room where I would constantly be groping around to try to find my way. I would keep bumping into things and moving away and suddenly find a clear spot, and then I could walk for a while. But there would soon be something else looming before me and I would get hurt again.

And after enough hurts, after the pain became so great that I couldn't bear it another moment, I finally surrendered. I surrendered to Alcohol.

And after years of addiction . . . suddenly a light shone on one object. And I saw hope! And I began to look within, and gradually other lights began to go on. I didn't have to stumble over the same objects anymore, at least not as hard! I began to see that my room had some defects and that if I could shine a light on each one and be willing to have them removed, then I had a chance of becoming happy and healthy and a real member of society! And as I began to see all the cluttered mess in my room, and gradually give each one up with willingness, to a Power Greater than myself for removal, my space got bigger and bigger, and I was able to walk around with more freedom!

When each light went on and I could see what was blocking my door to freedom, I made a list. It was often painful to see that these were the traits that were keeping me in that dark, black room. Sometimes it hurt so that I stayed in denial for a long time, not allowing myself to even look in certain corners, not wanting to have *that,* too! But when I crashed into the same object over and over again, when I knew that I didn't want to be black and blue anymore, when I remembered that when I was willing in the past and opened up the light, I got better. I reached a new level of willingness and was able to move on. And I was able to look at my defects, my imperfections, and gradually accept them without judgment.

And as all the objects became distinct and clear, I was able to move through the room with greater ease. I saw I had a *choice!* They didn't all go away. But just by accepting that they were there and not fighting with them and denying them anymore, I could be very happy in my room.

We keep learning that we have choices. We come to these points in the road and need to make a choice.

If your choice is for freedom and growth, remember . . .

A Star Is Lighting Your Path! Keep Going!

Once you see the obstacles in the room, you will discover that there is a door. And you have the key!

And that key is Willingness.

As you open the door, you will find a new path . . . in darkness. But now you have the lamp to light the way. You can get out of your self-made prison, your clutter, your darkness. You can find your blocks that have been keeping you from seeing the sun, from even shining like the sun!

You can transform these blocks into stepping stones to go on with your life!

Meditation is like putting a light on who we are. We have been in the dark for a long, long time. We have run away from ourselves for a long time. We have hidden ourselves from ourself and put out our lights. We have kept looking *out there* to find our answers, rather than *in here* . . . in our dark room.

As we begin to meditate our mind becomes quiet, and we begin to see ourselves as we really are.

At first one light might come on. And we begin to see a character defect or an old fear that might be blocking us from being our true selves. And we say "Oh! I didn't know I did that!" By seeing it, we can accept it. By accepting it we can decide what to do with it. We can then take responsibility for it. We can decide to own it or give it up.

We Can Take Action. Whereas before we always waited for something to happen to us or for us, we can now *do something for ourselves!!!*

We become actors instead of reactors!
We stop being victims and take charge of our lives!
We become responsible.

And then we can meditate some more and look some more and meditate some more and look some more; and the light keeps on getting brighter and brighter and the room keeps on getting bigger and bigger. And finally, one very beautiful day we will walk into our room and find it empty of all past baggage. Then a magic thing will happen. We will be as God has wanted us to be all along. We will walk into our own, very special room . . .

And we will be ourselves . . .
and we will be free!

"*When we discover the still, quiet place that lies within each of us, we can see it as a base to untangle ourselves from the doubt, indecision, ill health, guilt and other forms of old programming that result in confused and diffused actions.*"

Hallie Iglehart
Woman Spirit

This book is to introduce you to the valuable tools of Meditation, Positive Creative Visualization and Affirmations. It is combined in a program specifically designed for anyone who has difficulty with addictions or compulsions, but would certainly be useful for anyone who wishes to grow.

At the times when I have referred to alcohol, just substitute whatever fits you so that the tools in this book can have personal meaning in your life.

Before you even begin, please know . . . you cannot meditate wrong!

"You will reach down into your mind to a new place of safety. You will recognize you have reached it if you find a sense of deep peace . . . however briefly. Let go of all trivial things that churn and bubble on the surface of your mind, and reach down below them. There is a place in you where there is perfect peace . . . there is a place in you where nothing is impossible . . . there is a place in you where the strength of god . . . your higher power . . . lives."

Adapted from A Course in Miracles

Once you begin on this path, you will not want to stop. You have been walking in darkness too long. Lights will begin to go on for you and show you your truth.

You will get in touch with the blocks that keep you from being the terrific person you are!

The meditation we will do is based in Buddhism and is called Vipassana Meditation. It is a very simple meditation that will teach you single-pointed concentration and insight. It goes back over 2,500 years to the time of the Buddha, and is also known as Insight Meditation or Mindfulness.

Many of us have preconceived ideas of what meditation is. Maybe in our mind's eye we picture someone sitting yoga-style, body erect, in a white robe for hours and hours. This is only partly true. Vipassana Meditation *does* consist of the traditional sitting meditation. It also consists of a walking meditation to help us to learn awareness and concentration. It is ultimately a tool to learn to live in the *now*, to become aware, to become insightful all the hours of the day. It will help us to get in touch with a Power greater than ourselves, to find peace and serenity, and to help us to accept and then to love ourselves.

Meditation is an important tool for self-knowledge. It will enable us to see ourselves as we really are and allow us to let go of our character defects so that we can move on.

In the *Twelve Steps and Twelve Traditions* it states:

> *"When we refuse air, light and food, the body suffers. And when we turn away from meditation and prayer, we likewise deprive our minds, our emotions and our intuitions of vitally needed support. As the body can fail its purpose for lack of nourishment, so can the soul."*

> *Alcoholics Anonymous, World Service, Inc.*

And it goes on to say that "there is a direct linkage between self-examination, meditation and prayer." It says . . .

> **"Meditation is our step into the sun."**

It is therefore important to remember that while we are learning to meditate in a sitting position, while paying attention to our breathing, we are beginning to learn mindfulness. We will gain insight into our true nature.

The Power of Positive Thought

We are also going to learn how powerful our mind is, that we have the power and ability to turn our negative thinking around into positive thinking for positive results in our lives. We will learn that we are not victims of the universe. We will see that we no longer need to let persons, places or things control us.

Positive Creative Visualization

We will see that we can become who we want to be! We will learn how all goals begin in the mind and we can choose positive, rather than negative outcomes in our lives.

Affirmations

Through the powerful tools of affirmation we will learn how we can reprogram our negative tapes, no longer letting the guilt of the past or the fear of the future control us. By letting go of past programming, we will be fully alive in the *now!*

3

Spiritual Deprivation

*"Wanting is the urge for the next moment to
contain what this moment does not. When
there's wanting in the mind, that moment feels
incomplete. Wanting is seeking elsewhere.
Completeness is being right here."*

Stephen Levine

We reached out to people, places and things and thought
we would feel better. And that worked . . . for a while. When
that stopped working, some of us discovered alcohol or drugs,
food, work, sex or other addictions or dependencies. We
reached out for more and felt better, and wanted more and
more, and knew that was "it"! That made us feel better!
That made us feel "as good as" or "as attractive as" or "as
smart as" or whatever we needed to feel what we didn't feel.
For many of us it worked . . . for a long, long time.

When it stopped working, we tried new things or different
things or more-of-the-same things. We tried changing scenes
and friends and marriages and partners and sometimes towns
and states and countries.

We used our drinks and our pills and our food and our relationships to help us feel good if we felt bad, or better if we felt good. We used them for everything, even after they stopped working for us because we didn't know how to stop doing what we were doing. We didn't think we could stop because we thought our problem was everything else but our addictions.

We thought our problem was everything but ourselves. We thought it was all those people, places and things. We never knew how to take responsibility for our lives. We had never grown up.

As we chose to turn to these dependencies as the solution to feel better, we were actually making a choice away from growing up, away from maturity, away from taking responsibility for our own lives. All that reaching out to find our happiness gave us moments of satisfaction that didn't last.

. BIG eMPTY HOLE

It was as if we had a big empty hole in the middle of our stomachs that needed constant filling to feel good. If we put alcohol or drugs or food into it, it would feel good and there would be no pain. We would numb all those feelings of guilt and discomfort and insecurity. Or we turned to other people to take responsibility for our happiness.

We didn't know who was living inside us!

When we give up these dependencies, that big hole begins rapidly to be refilled with:

Pain	Fear	Resentments	Guilt
Doubt	Pride	Anger	Self-pity

And we think, "If I feel this bad, who needs it!" Here we were in this new and frightening state. We finally admitted that we were powerless over our addictions.

"...meditation quiets and clears
the mind..."

4

Medication To Meditation

"The longest journey is the journey inward, for he who has chosen his destiny has started upon his quest for the source of his being."

Dag Hammarsjkold

All the feelings we had suppressed for years and years pushed up, spilling out and over and around us, surrounding us like a hot air balloon, and giving us no space to breathe. We felt raw and alone and afraid.

After taking all our medication, anesthetizing and drugging our senses, we now needed something to be gentle with our frail and vulnerable selves.

Meditation was just the thing!

But how? With so much turmoil and stress how were we to sit quietly and meditate? With so much fear and guilt and self-loathing, how can we possibly stay calm enough to sit long enough to meditate?

So far we have been *talking* about meditation, now let's experience it for a few moments!

5

Basic Sitting Meditation Instructions

How To Dress

Wear comfortable, loose clothing. Be sure it is appropriate for the weather. You will soon be sitting for a long time, and it will be best to dress so that you are not conscious of warmth or cold.

How To Sit

Where you sit is less important than how you sit. It is important to have your back and your neck straight and your chin slightly up.

If you can sit yoga-style with your legs crossed in a lotus or semi-lotus position, you will have the best balance for longer periods of sitting. At first this may seem very uncomfortable and your body might not want to sit that way. You may wish to get a book of yoga exercises and learn how to stretch your body so that it can be comfortable in that position. The more you try it, the easier it will get.

If you cannot learn the lotus or the semi-lotus, you can sit crossed-legged Indian style.

If you find that you cannot manage this position either, you can sit in a chair with your feet on the floor. Be sure your back and your neck are straight and your chin is slightly up.

The Perfect Place

There are basically three types of places to meditate.

First, there is your home where you spend much of your time. If this is in a family setting, try to find time for yourself when it is most quiet. Ask that this time be respected by all and that you are not interrupted. Know that you are not asking for any special favors. You are no more special than the other members of the family, but you deserve this time just as others deserve it.

It might be necessary to get up earlier than the rest of the family. (If you think that this will be difficult for you to do, read the section on setting your personal clock.) You will be amazed at the ease and the joy you will receive in being in charge of your own time.

If your current home is shared with others who are not your family, such as a hospital, treatment center, halfway house or group home, the same suggestions as stated above apply to you here. It might be more of a challenge to find that quiet time, but it can be done if you really want it.

Also know that you do not have to meditate alone. It can be a very beautiful, powerful experience to meditate with a roommate, a spouse, a lover, a friend or a group of people, just as long as all involved are committed to peace and quiet in meditation.

Meditation can be done outside . . . at the beach or in the woods or in your own backyard. Often it is not the quietest spot because noises that are absolutely out of your control, such as squirrels, birds, crashing waves or strong winds, can be very disturbing. But if you are concentrated enough to just let these noises be, this also can be a most rewarding experience.

Secondly, meditating with a group while taking lessons is usually a more controlled environment where noises are at a minimum and space is comfortable. This is a good way to learn and a good way to practice, but it is important to realize that this controlled environment cannot always be duplicated at home. If you expect it, disappointments will occur. There is usually more power found when meditating with a group.

Third is the experience of meditating at a retreat, where the conditions are designed to be as perfect as possible. We need to know that it is not practical to expect to duplicate them in real life. When we return to the reality of our everyday lives, we need to learn how to be in charge of our own time and our own space and accept the reality of our present conditions.

Experience Meditation By Following Your Breath

Sit comfortably and relax. If someone can read this to you, it would be most helpful. But if you are doing this by yourself, that's fine too. Just read this over first and then follow the instructions. It might take a few times to read them, but they are simple, and you will get used to them.

Close your eyes and begin to breathe in and out. Don't try to control your breathing in any way. Just let it be natural.

Get To Know the Characteristics of your Breath

For the next two or three minutes just close your eyes, sit quietly and be aware of your breathing.

Be aware of your breath as it goes in and as it goes out of your nostrils. Don't follow your breath all the way down or control or force your breathing. In the beginning it helps to make mental notes of *rising/falling* or *in/out*. This aids in keeping your mind on your breathing.

Notice your breath as it goes in and as it goes out. See if you can feel if it is cool or warm, long or short. Don't try to make it something that it is not. Don't change it. Just let it be and observe it. Notice if it is shallow or deep. Notice if it changes.

If thoughts come in, just let them be and go back to your breathing.

If feelings come up, just notice them and go back to your breathing.

If you experience an itch or a pain, try not to move. Bring your attention to that area of your body and see if it doesn't go away.

If you get lost in a thought or a daydream, just notice that you got lost and bring your attention gently back to your breathing. It would be helpful to make a mental note of what it was that took you away from your breathing.

Now plan to spend a few more minutes *experiencing* meditation.

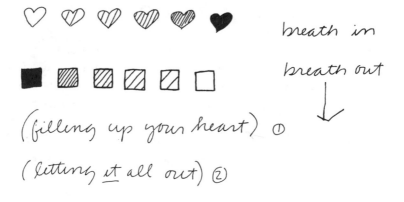

Let your body relax.

Feel relaxation flow through your head
    and your neck.

Relax your eyes
    and your mouth
        and your head.

Feel tension leave the back of your neck
    and your shoulders.
Let relaxation pour down your arms
    and your hands
        and tension flow out through your
            fingers.

Your back and your chest are relaxing
    and you are feeling relaxation in your
        stomach
            and your hips and
                your pelvis.

Relaxation is pouring down your thighs
    and your hips
        and your knees.

Your legs are feeling so relaxed
    as are your ankles
        and your feet
            and your toes.

Now go back and check your body for any left-over
    tightness and bring relaxation to them.

And then return your attention to your
    breathing
        as you breathe in
            and you breathe out . . .
                as you breathe in
                    and you breathe out.

Know that as you breathe in,
    you are breathing in positive energy.
        You are breathing in power
            and love
                and goodness.

And as you breathe out, you are exhaling

all the negative elements that block you
from your Higher Power.

You are breathing out tension
and anger
and resentments.

Breathe in and breathe out . . .

Breathe in
and breathe out.

Now just be with your breathing for a while . . .

And when you are ready, count to five very slowly before opening your eyes and come back to the room.

It Is Absolutely Normal To Have Thoughts!

Just notice them and go back to your breathing . . .
Notice your thoughts and return to your breathing . . .
Bring your attention back to your breathing . . .
If you notice yourself planning for something in the future, just notice it and gently go back to your breathing . . .
If you notice that you are letting in a past memory, just notice that and return to your breathing . . .

There Will Always Be Noises

As with thoughts, just notice the noises and go back to your breathing. Don't try to block them out. Don't resist them. Just hear them and bring your attention back to your breathing.

Notice . . . Don't Resist or Struggle

Whatever comes up for you, just let it be and go back to your breathing. The more you practice this, the easier it will become.

The more you struggle with a thought, the more it will stay in your mind and take over. You will see that if you just notice it, it will gradually disappear.

Spend a good 10 or 15 minutes with this exercise and then very gradually open your eyes and return to the room.

How Long To Practice Sitting Meditation

It is important to remember that we are learning a very simple meditation based on a Buddha Meditation called Vispassana or Insight Meditation, and that it is more than a sitting meditation. It is a meditation to gain insight. It is a meditation to gain awareness.

To meditate just once in a while will have little, if any, value. But if you begin to practice it on a daily basis, you will find extraordinary results! You can discover Healthy and Natural highs and good feelings that you looked for in alcohol and drugs or other dependencies. And most important you will begin to know that there really is a terrific person living inside you after all, someone you just have not yet had the privilege of meeting.

Begin with as little as 10 minutes in the morning and if possible, 10 minutes at night. You can gradually increase this. Even 10 minutes a day, done on a daily basis will produce results.

Learning To Be In The Now

You will find a great value in this kind of meditation for a slowing down, a relaxation and a beginning to see how your mind works *from moment to moment* . . .

Take one simple routine that you do in the day, such as taking a shower or brushing your teeth. Notice everything that you feel and see and experience while doing it. Be with yourself and your feelings. If your mind starts planning, notice that it is planning and not being in the *now* and bring it back. Notice how the water feels on your body. If your mind begins to let the past into the *now*, just notice how the past is interfering with your *now* and notice how your skin feels as you dry yourself or the water sounds as it hits the tub.

When we were into escaping, it was impossible to know what we were experiencing in the *now* because our *now* was not real! *We were never in the now! We chose our addiction instead of reality.*

You are learning to be in charge of your mind.

You are learning to experience the present.

You are learning to choose the reality of the now.

You will find your strength within you;
In places deep inside where you have not
yet dared to visit. Know that you have
all that you need to do all that is good
and right in your life today.

6

Finding Your Path
For Peace

"Once you plant deep the longing for peace
Confusion leaves of itself."

Seng Ts'an,
Believing in Mind

For so many years it seemed as if my life was always about struggle. I had struggled to get sober and struggled through a painful divorce. I had struggled to let go of a losing business and struggled to start a new one. I had struggled to develop an alcoholism program and struggled to keep it going. And it seemed that no matter how hard I tried or worked or studied or prayed or did what I was told to do, or what I thought I was supposed to do, the struggle continued.

Many times my moods went so deep that I thought I was going to be in depression forever. It had been suggested that I might be a manic depressive. I had been diagnosed as one in my drinking years and put on lithium while still drinking by a psychiatrist who knew nothing about alcoholism but was committed to 'curing' me regardless. The results were horrendous and I found myself at a zero level of emotion and energy. I thank God I had enough sense to take myself off the lithium, knowing that I would prefer to take the consequences of a depression if I could just feel alive again. It was suggested off and on during my recovery that I go back on lithium again or take an antidepressant. I kept on holding off, believing that if I followed the 12-step program, I would clear up. It helped me throughout this period to know that Bill Wilson, the founder of Alcoholics Anonymous, went in and out of depressions, and that they got further and further apart the longer he stayed sober.

One day a friend received a birthday present which I immediately took over for the next six months. That book remained stuck to me like a magnet and said "This is it! This is what you have been looking for!" It was entitled *God Makes the Rivers To Flow* and consisted of passages for meditation selected by Eknath Easwaran.

I read this book a number of mornings and began to feel very peaceful and had a sense I was on a new direction. Suddenly one morning I read . . .

"Once you plant deep the longing for peace
Confusion leaves of itself."

And a light went on for me! A feeling of relief flooded through me that I remember only feeling once before when I entered an alcoholism recovery program for the first time. I knew the battle was over. I knew I had found the answer. I knew I was at choice.

I had thought I had found *"The Answer"* many other times in my life by way of other books. But what was different this time was that even though I always knew that God was the answer, I had never known how to just let my life go enough to listen to God.

This time it became very clear that all I had to do was make a decision, really want peace and it would come. I needed to know it on a deeper level . . . inside. I never felt that before. I knew it was not only possible, but I knew that I would be shown the way.

I had learned Transcendental Meditation (TM) five years earlier and had practiced it faithfully every morning for twenty minutes, not missing a day. It was very helpful in that it helped me relax and taught me a discipline that I never had before. But I felt as if there must be more to meditation or maybe I just was not getting out of meditation what there was to get. But still I practiced it daily, somewhat afraid to give it up, afraid I would miss something.

Each day before I meditated, I read the quote about confusion, continuing to reinforce this knowledge for myself and being open to hear how this could happen.

A great deal did happen from that day to now. Most of it is a story for another time. By willingness to let God work in my life and willingness to learn to let go, I was introduced to A Course in Miracles, which was and still is a profound influence in my life. I found out that I was just who I wanted to be, a teacher of miracles, and I was to learn to become much better at my job.

I first learned about A Course in Miracles at a workshop when I was working towards my masters degree. The name itself drew me like a magnet, just as I had been drawn to other powerful forces in my life. "A Course in Miracles," I remember saying to myself, "can't be said without smiling." My sobriety was a miracle. My life in sobriety was truly a miracle. I believed in miracles and had even designed a bumper sticker that said *Expect Miracles*. Needless to say I went to that two-hour workshop to find out about A Course in Miracles.

I found out that it was a program based on Forgiveness and Atonement, or at-one-ment, and that it fit right into the twelve-step program I had already been practicing in my life. Part of it felt very "heavy" to me in that it seemed based on Christianity. Being Jewish by birth, although I did not practice Judaism in my daily life, I did not feel this was the direction in which I wanted to go. But on the other side of it, the forgiveness and atonement fascinated me, as did the fact that it kept on referring to miracles. I decided I wanted to learn more about it.

A dear friend gave me the three volumes for my graduation. Volume one is a text book consisting of 622 pages, volume two a workbook for students with one lesson for each day of the year and volume three is a manual for teachers. The instructions found in the introduction are as follows:

> *"This is a course in miracles. It is a required course. Only the time you take it is voluntary. Free will does not mean you can establish the curriculum. It means only that you can elect what you want to take at any given time. The course does not aim at teaching the meaning of love, for that is beyond what can be taught. It does aim, however, at removing the blocks to the awareness of love's presence, which is your natural inheritance. The opposite of love is fear, but what is all-encompassing can have no opposite.*
>
> *"This course can therefore be summed up very simply in this way:*
>
> > *Nothing real can be threatened.*
> > *Nothing unreal exists.*
> *"Herein lies the peace of God."*

As often happens when we become open for our next step on our Spiritual Path, more answers begin to appear. A catalogue from a local center soon arrived listing a weekend workshop on *A Course in Miracles*. By this time I was on page 322 and eager to learn more. the workshop helped to clarify the teachings and explained how the course began.

Helen Schaffer, a psychologist, became what is known as a scribe for a voice she heard in her head. She had no other explanation for this knowledge and began her writing in 1965, taking eight years to complete it. The books were published in 1975.

I began adding the *Course in Miracles* to my daily meditation, another miracle in self discipline. I did this by turning my will and my life over to a power greater than myself and meaning it, as much as I was able.

I became willing to give up two stores which I had struggled to keep alive long after they served their usefulness.

Hugh Prather had written in his book *I Touch the Earth, The Earth Touches Me:*

"My growth does not seem to be a matter of learning new lessons, but of learning the old lessons again and again. The wisdom doesn't change, only the situations. Another kind of 'being in touch': being in touch with the situation, being open to the signal that 'enough is enough.' Events are not controlled by my will. It is irrelevant how I want things to go; the question is how are they going?

"Surely this must be an ancient proverb: If the situation is killing you, get the hell out."

When I was finally introduced to Vipassana Meditation, I finally found the vehicle to find the "more" I had been looking for in meditation. It ties in perfectly with all the recovery programs for anyone addicted to anything.

7

Beginning Your Journey

∴

*"You are going to find
a star to light your path."*

A Course in Miracles

You are now ready to begin your journey on your Spiritual Path within. You have read enough to know that it is a gentle path. So without any further delay, let's begin!

To gain the full benefits of **Meditation Plus,** a small period of time each day is needed. To expect to grow without taking action will just lead to frustration and eventually lack of interest. So be good to yourself. Make a commitment to grow and develop on your Spiritual Path so that you can know the joy of living and develop your personal power.

Take your time. Put aside time for yourself every day. Find a place where you know your privacy will be respected.

8

Spiritual Prescriptions for Growth and Change

*"I am fortunate indeed! I have been granted the
wealth of another day of life."*

Anthony de Mello

I. PASSIVE STEPS

Meditation

- Reduce stress
- Quiet and clear the Mind
- Which leads to . . .

Awareness and Insight

- Begin to see what is between us and God
- Begin to see who we really are
- Shine the light on stumbling blocks
- Listen with clarity
- Begin to hear God's will for us
- Find Peace in our inner sanctuary

II. ACTIVE STEPS

Acceptance
- Accept ourselves as we are, as we see ourselves
- Forgive ourselves and others so that we can be . . .
- Free from yesterday

Empty Ourselves
- Become empty before we can refill
- Forgive ourselves and others
- Let go of the past

Healing
- Unblock our natural power

Visualize (Fill)
- Set new goals

Energize
- Feel the power of your inner guide
- Feel the power of the universe
- Unblock our natural power
- Feel the power of our words

Symbolize (Fill)
- Create new automatic reflexes
- New positive buttons to be pushed

Affirm (Fill and Energize)
- Create a new self-image and own it
- Discipline ourselves with self-esteem

Action
- Easily and effortlessly

9

Meditation

*"We will want the good that is in all of us,
even in the worst of us, to flower and grow.
Most certainly we shall need bracing air and
abundance of food. But first of all we shall
want sunlight; nothing much can grow in the
dark. Meditation is our step out into the sun."*

Twelve Steps and Twelve Traditions
Alcoholics Anonymous

Begin with a minimum of 10 minutes each morning and
each night. If you find it absolutely impossible to do it twice
a day, do it in the morning. That will set you up in the
right frame of mind for the rest of your day. Gradually
increase the length of time of each sitting to at least 20
minutes.

Reread Chapter 5 for the Basic Meditation Instructions
on how to sit, where to sit and what to wear.

**I am now going to repeat the Basic Meditation. This
is how to meditate each morning and each night. Before
any other exercise in this book always begin with this basic
meditation.**

For the next two or three minutes, just close your eyes and sit quietly and be aware of your breathing.

Be aware of your breath as it goes in and as it goes out of your nostrils. Don't follow your breath all the way down or control or force your breathing. In the beginning it helps to make mental notes of *rising/falling* or *in/out*. This aids in keeping your mind on your breathing.

Just notice your breath, as it goes in and as it goes out. See if you can notice if it is cool or warm, long or short. Don't try to make it something that it is not. Don't change it. Just let it be and observe it. Notice if it is shallow or deep. Notice if it changes.

If thoughts come in, just let them be and go back to your breathing.

If feelings come up, just notice them and go back to your breathing.

If you experience an itch or a pain, try not to move. Bring your attention to that area of your body and see if it goes away.

If you become lost in a thought or a daydream, just notice that you are lost and bring your attention back to your breathing. It would be helpful to make a mental note of what it was that took you away from your breathing.

Now plan to spend a few more minutes experiencing meditation.

Let your body relax.

Feel relaxation flow through your head
and your neck.

Relax your eyes
and your mouth
and your head.

Feel tension leave the back of your neck
and your shoulders.

Let relaxation pour down your arms
and your hands
and tension flow out through your
fingers.

Your back and your chest are relaxing
and you are feeling relaxation in your
stomach
and your hips and
your pelvis.

Relaxation is pouring down your thighs
and your hips
and your knees.

Your legs are feeling so relaxed
as are your ankles
and your feet
and your toes.

Now go back and check your body for any leftover
tightness and bring relaxation to them.

And then return your attention to your
breathing
as you breathe in
and you breathe out . . .
as you breathe in
and you breathe out.

Know that as you breathe in,
  you are breathing in positive energy.
    You are breathing in power
      and love
        and good.

And as you breathe out you are exhaling
  all the negative elements that block you
    from your Higher Power.

You are breathing out tension
  and anger
    and resentments.

Breathe in and breathe out . . .

Breathe in
  and breathe out.

Now just be with your breathing for a while . . .
And when you are ready, count to three very slowly before opening your eyes and come back to the room.
Remember that it is normal to have thoughts.
Just notice them and go back to your breathing.
Notice your thoughts and return to your breathing.
Bring your attention back to your breathing. If you notice yourself planning for something in the future, just notice it and go back to your breathing.
If you notice that you are letting in a past memory, just notice that and return to your breathing.
And it is normal to hear noises. As with the thoughts, just notice the noises and go back to your breathing. Don't try to block them out. Don't resist them. Just hear them and bring your attention back to your breathing.
Whatever comes up for you, just let it be and go back to your breathing. The more you practice this, the easier it will become.
The more you struggle with a thought, the more it will stay in your mind and take over. You will see that if you just notice it, it will gradually disappear.

Spend a good 10 to 15 minutes with this exercise. And then very gradually open your eyes and return to the room.

> "A person always finds when he begins to practice meditation that all sorts of problems are brought out. Any hidden aspects of your personality are brought out into the open, for the simple reason that for the first time, you are allowing yourself to see your state of mind as it is."
>
> Chogyam Trungpa

" begin to accept whatever comes up as a learning experience."

Awareness and Insight

Begin to bring awareness to everything you do. Do not judge! Just bring awareness. Notice yourself. Get to know yourself. Begin the process of self-acceptance and self-love.

As you begin to develop the regular habit of meditation, you will begin to hear the conversations that continually take place in your mind. You will begin to become aware of your *self-talk*, the things that you tell yourself. You will begin to hear negative tapes and how they reinforce a poor self-image. And you will gradually begin to learn that these negative tapes that come from your past experiences are deeply embedded in your subconscious and keep you stuck, unable to move forward.

As Henry Ford once said,

*"Whether you think you can or can't,
you're right!"*

And as your mind begins to wander, notice what does take you away from the *now*, from the *moment* and what you are doing in the moment. Do not judge but learn from what you see. Notice whether you are letting past thoughts or feelings rob you of your now. Or does future planning and worrying keep coming in? Maybe fear or guilt or anxiety takes you away from *being alive in the moment*.

Just notice what is happening. And jot down what comes up as a *block*.

Visualization

Visualizations are excellent tools to use to turn around the negative tapes you often hear and see into positive ones. They can help you begin to move toward becoming the full person that you want to be. You can create new goals and actually visualize yourself already achieving them in your mind. By creating a positive new picture in your mind and then letting your body actually experience the feelings *as if it has actually happened*, you will be able to create new positive experiences with more and more ease.

Used regularly, visualizations can be powerful tools to help us act in new ways. As we will learn later in this book, our bodies cannot discern the difference between real and imaged situations. They will believe what our minds imagine, thereby responding to real situations and imagined situations in exactly the same way.

They are like dress rehearsals. If you imagine a situation often enough, then by the time that you actually find yourself in that situation, it will be familiar to you. For example, if you imagine that you have confidence in a future situation, your body will respond with confidence when it occurs. If you do this often enough, you can form new habits so that your mind and your body will respond as you choose in any actual situation.

Affirmations

Affirmations are another powerful tool for changing negative tapes into positive ones. Used daily, you will find that an entirely new attitude will lead to a positive and wonderful way of life!

An affirmation is a positive thought that we imagine as if it were true in the now. If we say it and feel it with conviction, it will *become* true. An affirmation can be written or stated positively. But if we write our affirmation and then read it aloud, we are using our eyes, our ears and our bodies to affirm the new messages we are telling ourselves.

As in visualization, affirmations are stated as if they were happening now, as if they were real. They affirm your visualization. They work when they are said with *conviction*, stated as if they are true in the *now*, are said with *energy*, and are *repeated* at least 10 times a day for 21 days. A few examples of affirmations that might be helpful for you are . . .

I deserve to let good things happen in my life today!

I am moving towards the right job for me.

I am meeting people who are positive and supportive in my life.

We will be going into more details about affirmations and visualizations later.

This is just the beginning of moving toward personal freedom and reaching your full potential!

(These affirmations at the end of each chapter are suggestions only. Try them out and see how they feel to you. Say them aloud and notice how you feel as you say the words. You can change them, if you like and create your own. You will be reading more about affirmations in Chapter 31.)

Your Affirmation

**"Today I am beginning my Spiritual Path
to recovery."**

10

Excuses

"It is a mistake to think
that the sadhana
(meditation)
cannot be practiced for lack of time.
The real cause is agitation of the mind."

Swami Brahmananda,
Discipline Monastique

"As meditation deepens, compulsions, cravings and fits of emotion begin to lose their power to dictate our behavior. We see clearly that choices are possible: we can say yes or we can say no. It is profoundly liberating."

Eknath Easwaran

There are always excuses as to why one can't meditate. The two most common that I hear are "I don't have time!" and "I can't because I think too much!"

We do not have time to say: "We do not have time!"

People can be rushing around from dawn to midnight, but really believe that they do not have 20 minutes in the morning and 20 minutes in the evening to be good to themselves, just 40 minutes that would be a positive influence on the rest of their 24 hours.

I rarely hear anyone say that it won't work. I rarely hear anyone use the excuse that they don't like it when they do meditate and that it doesn't make them feel better.

> *"Meditation is a form of acknowledging your connection with the spirit of universal love, and it allows a sense of peace and love to flood your being. The tranquility that follows stays with you, reducing stress and promoting a state of awareness throughout the day."*
>
> *"We become what we imagine, positive or negative."*
>
> Ruth Ross

Therefore if you imagine you haven't enough time, you haven't enough time! If you imagine you have enough time, you have enough time!

> *"We cannot leave the trap until we know we are in it."*
>
> Marilyn Ferguson

I never thought I had time to meditate either. I was always too busy. I always had too much to do. And it is an objection that I hear over and over again. I think what finally happened for me was that I heard a challenge. I had been trying for many years to take a few minutes each morning to at least read inspirational or spiritual passages to help me begin my day in a positive, loving, spiritual frame of mind. But I couldn't do it with any regularity.

I had always been a person who hated routine. I thought that anyone who did the same things on the same day, each week or each month (for instance, laundry on Monday) was profoundly boring. And I thought I would be bored to death if I lived my life in that fashion. I think this came from an old stubborn, childish habit of "I want to do what I want to do when I want to do it, and not because my mother [or father or teacher or whoever] told me to do it!" And yet I was in a conflict at a level that I did not like to admit even to myself. The people who did their laundry on Mondays and their shopping on Tuesday *always got their laundry and shopping done!!!* I, on the other hand, might have had the best plans, but was easily influenced by a call for a bridge game or a few beers when I was in school with studying to do. Many an "all-nighter" took the place of studying for an exam.

I remember even in college resenting and blaming my mother when I saw one of my classmates wash her hair every Wednesday night. Boring as I thought that was, I remember thinking that if only my mother had insisted that I do chores routinely, I would have had better habits by the time I entered college. And I wouldn't have wasted so much time playing bridge.

I rationalized that I was a creative person and could not possibly do things on the same day every week or my mind would be in a box and limited. I think I also associated routines with cleaning the house and doing so-called 'woman's work' and I knew at some level of my consciousness that I never wanted to spend my life like that. My mother's life had been devoted to her family and her home, and it seemed as if she were always doing something for someone else, sacrificing her own life and wishes. I always vowed I would never be like her.

I did go on to many other "creative" things with my life. Over the years alcohol became more and more a part of my life. I used it to relax, to celebrate, to dance, to be one of the group, to deal with anything uncomfortable, to dull the pain or the boredom; in short, I used it for just about everything that came up. It was always there for me or so I thought. Gradually it stopped working for me. And one day I knew finally that I couldn't stop drinking, even though I desperately wanted to do so. Somehow I needed to get help to stop before I died or lost my mind or both.

In the end I was blessed to find the help that I needed, to find the people who would help me and save my life. I finally found people who had been where I had been and had learned how to live a happy, fulfilling life without using a drink or a substitute. I let the grace of God enter my life.

After several years of being sober and hearing words like prayer and meditation of which I knew nothing, I was very ready to learn more. I had put down the drink, grown in many ways and made a beginning at being the person that I wanted to be.

Just as I had needed help to stop drinking, I soon knew that I would need help to learn how to meditate. A friend knew someone who was a teacher of Transcendental Meditation (TM), and I was ready for structured meditation. I knew I could not do it on my own. I wanted to grow. I wanted to feel the peace promised. I was ready to change. I no longer accepted my scattered way of doing things.

My TM instructor mentioned that he had found that people who have self-respect and a positive self-image have a far greater chance to practice TM on a regular basis. He said that those who did not like themselves would not take the time or effort to discipline themselves to do something that would ultimately make them feel good about themselves. I remember very clearly thinking that I wanted to feel good about myself, no matter what. I reasoned that if on days that I did not *want* to take the time, it meant that I didn't like myself so I would refuse to let that get in my way. I was determined that if not liking myself was one of my problems, I was going to act as if that were not true. And it worked.

Up until then my head began working and planning two hours before I got out of bed. I used to try to figure everything out before getting up in the morning. I would think about my problems, try to work them all out and go over them and over them and over them. Fears would come, and I did not know why I was afraid and did not know how to stop them. Many mornings I would become so overwhelmed that I was on the verge of anxiety attacks by the time I was brushing my teeth. The minute my feet hit the floor I was rushed and scattered and never knew what was wrong with me. I was constantly trying to improve the way I did things, and never knowing how.

After I learned TM, I began to read about meditation as soon as I awoke each morning. I would then meditate for 20 minutes as I had been taught, using a mantra. (A mantra is a word given by the TM teacher, which we are to say over and over again, to quiet the mind. We have to make a vow that we are never to share this word with anyone.) I learned to quiet down my thoughts and achieve relative calm. I finally experienced a peaceful state of mind while sober.

I meditated every morning for five years! That was a remarkable feat for one who hated routines! It became something I could not do without. If I had to catch an early morning plane and could not meditate first thing in the morning, I would always find time to catch up and do it as soon as possible.

Everyone has to find their own path, the type of meditation that fits them best. Transcendental Meditation I am sure is perfect for many people. But gradually for me I knew there was still something missing. I knew intuitively there was more, and I wanted it. I also had a problem with my commitment to secrecy. Since I could not share the word for my mantra with anyone, I could never teach anyone else how to do TM. And I was feeling a growing need to teach meditation to others, to share the good that I was feeling with other people.

As part of my daily routine I prayed every morning that I would not take a drink or a pill or a substitute that day. I always asked God to remove everything that was in my way of serving Him/Her. I knew I had a mission, a calling in life, and that at my present level of conscious contact with God I was only partially able to fulfill it.

As I continued to practice, my morning craziness lessened. My scatteredness still went on, however, and I was still into a life of struggle that I deeply wanted to change. I knew the answer was in achieving greater spirituality, but I did not yet know how to reach it.

"there are times when we have to go through layers and layers of insight to find the answer."

But I continued to struggle, and without going into a lot of details at this point, I found myself in a position where I was, for the second time in my life, responsible for a business that was in a great deal of debt, and I was again struggling to find a way to keep it going. All the fears that were in my life the first time kept coming up for me. I knew that in the first situation I was already an alcoholic and was in no position to handle anything rationally. But here I was sober for 10 years and doing the same things again! What was wrong with me? Was I a masochist? Was I afraid of success? Or was it failure that I feared?

I thought I needed to learn more so I entered college to earn my Master's degree in Human Service Administration. I had really wanted to do my master's project on creativity in recovery, but it was strongly suggested by the faculty that since my business was in such a precarious condition, I had better take this time to learn what to do about it. I had been working with recovering alcoholic women for the majority of my recovery. I really loved what I was doing but knew that if I continued to do what I was doing the way that I was doing it, it would ruin me. I was close to "burn out."

Meditation had helped but I still didn't seem to know how to change. Confusion continued in my life. Mornings were still the same struggle of trying to figure it out. People said to "let go, let God." I tried to do this but at the same time I continued to think and try to figure it out, to "solve" everything.

This confusion finally led to a new direction of meditation. I learned the basics of the meditation we are learning here, Vapassana Meditation, which is basically a meditation of *insight* and *awareness* and this new discipline became very important in my life.

> "A healed mind does not plan. It carries out the plans it receives through listening to Wisdom that is not its own. It waits until it has been taught what should be done and then proceeds to do it. It does not depend upon itself for anything except its adequacy to fulfill the plans assigned to it."
>
> A Course in Miracles

Your Affirmation

"Nothing can stop me from growing today!"

11

So You Think You're Different Because You Think Too Much

*"God does not require from novices prayer completely
free from distractions. Do not despond when your
thought is distracted, but remain calm, and
unceasingly restore your mind to itself."*

St. John of the Ladder

The other most common excuse is that most people I have talked to, or taught meditation to, think they are *different*. I certainly did! I always thought that something was wrong with me because I couldn't make my mind stop talking. I remember lying in bed as a child and not being able to get thoughts out of my mind. I even remember thinking "OK, I will not think anymore. I am thinking about thinking and I will not think about thinking anymore. I am thinking about not thinking, and I will not think about not thinking anymore." And this went on and on hour after hour and night after night.

Not until I heard other people speak about the same craziness did I realize that I was not alone. And it was not until I began to study meditation seriously that I discovered these experiences were pretty much universal. Every book on meditation that I read referred to this steady chatter that goes on in our minds. And I suddenly saw that if so many were writing about it and spending so much time on it, then everyone must experience it.

I think that the reason that I didn't know already was because I had finally found a way many years ago to put this chatter to rest. Alcohol first quieted my mind and gave me peace. And then pills served to do the same. And when they no longer worked, I thought I was crazy.

And the blessing that happened for me was that I finally . . .

> *Came to believe that a power greater than myself*
> *could restore me to sanity.*
>
> *Twelve Steps and Twelve Traditions*

So we learn that everyone has thoughts. We are not unique. For at least 2500 years people who have begun to practice meditation began to see that they have thoughts that control their minds.

And the first impulse is to say "I can't. My mind won't stop. I can't be still." Please know that I said this. Please know that millions have thought this. And most important, please know that *you can stop them and be still.*

Suzuki Roshi in *Zen's Mind, Beginner's Mind* writes:

> *"When you are practicing Zazen meditation, do not try to stop your thinking. Let it stop by itself. If something comes into your mind, let it come in and let it go out. It will not stay long. When you try to stop your thinking, it means that you are bothered by it. Do not be bothered by anything."*

So when thoughts come in, just notice them. Do not judge them as good or bad, right or wrong. Just notice them and go back to your breathing. When you think of something from your past, just notice that you are letting your *past* interfere with your *now* and go back to your breathing. When you find yourself planning, just notice that you are letting your *future* take over your *now* and go back to your breathing. This is going to teach you how your mind works. You will grow in the knowledge of yourself and as you become more and more aware, at deeper and deeper levels, you will begin to find peace.

> *"The practice of meditation will open us gradually to more and more energy of the universe. If we remember the highest wisdom (that energy and love are one) this journey will be without fear . . . With love you are more open to the energy. Then you will grow in power, the power of love. You are on your way home."*

Ram Dass
Journey of Awakening

Your Affirmation

**"I am learning to accept ALL my thoughts
as a beautiful part of who I am."**

12

Action Steps

"We must begin our practice by walking the
narrow path of simplicity . . . before we can
walk upon the open highway of compassionate
action . . . And only after our highway journey
is well on its way need we concern ourselves
about how to dance in the fields."

Chogyam Trungpa

Now that we have moved through discussing the most common excuses for not meditating, know that there will be many more excuses that come up for you. This is very normal. Self-discipline is not easy for anyone who has not yet experienced its benefits. And as we have been learning, our minds will tell us anything to avoid discomfort. As addicts we are used to looking for the easier, softer way and avoiding hard work and possible pain.

So as we hear our minds tell us that we would rather be anywhere else or doing anything else, know that it is just our minds talking and we do not have to listen.

Meditation is essential if we are to grow and develop a deeper conscious contact with our Higher Power. It is essential to getting to the truth of who we are and who we can be. Meditation is essential if we are to find peace and truth and serenity. But it is not everything. It is not enough. It must be accompanied by action.

I remember a wonderful story that Father Martin told about a young man who wanted to be a doctor. Every night he prayed to God that he would become a doctor. Every night for years he prayed that God would make him a doctor. Finally, after years and years of praying and waiting, he told God that he had been waiting so long and had prayed so much and nothing had happened. The young man asked God why hadn't he made him a doctor? Finally God answered. The young man heard a booming voice from above saying, "Go to medical school!"

I love that story! It says it all about the action that we need to take. There is no Great Power moving people, places and things around for us so that we can just sit and meditate and go to the mailbox and receive a check. I have heard so many people say that if God wanted them to have a job, they would have one. And they sit year after year complaining about welfare and social security and unemployment and stay stuck in waiting for God to do it for them. In the Big Book of Alcoholics Anonymous wonderful promises are made that people will realize as a result of working the twelve steps of the program . . .

> We are going to know a new freedom and a new happiness.
>
> We will not regret the past or wish to shut the door on it.
>
> We will comprehend the word "serenity" and we will know peace.
>
> No matter how far down the scale we have gone, we will see how our experience will benefit others.
>
> That feeling of uselessness and self-pity will disappear.
>
> We will lose interest in selfish things and gain interest in our fellows.

Self-seeking will slip away.

Our whole attitude and outlook on life will change.

Fear of people and economic insecurity will leave us.

*We will intuitively know how to handle situations
which used to baffle us.*

*We will suddenly realize that God is doing for us
what we could not do for ourselves.*

Are these extravagant promises? We think not. They are being fulfilled among us — sometimes quickly, sometimes slowly. They will always materialize *if we work for them.*

We are learning to practice our meditation. We are working very diligently and learning and have meditated when we were sick and when we wanted to sleep and when we would have rather been doing something else. We have meditated when people have laughed at us, and have meditated when our friends didn't understand us and thought we were strange.

The important thing is we have got in touch with our source of power, our God, the creative energies of the universe. Now, how can we make that work in our lives? How can we become "doctors"?

We must become active, that is how. We have to do things that might be uncomfortable. We have to take all the steps that we can to free ourselves from the past so that we can live in the now and be fully alive!

GO FOR IT!!!

Your Affirmation

*"Today I am willing to meditate . . .
whether I feel like it or not!"*

13

Living in the NOW

*". . . a joy will open our
hearts like a flower,
enabling us to enter
the world of reality."*

Thich Nhat Hanh

To live in the peace of the now would truly be a miracle for those of us who have experienced fear of the future and shame and guilt of the past. Wouldn't it be a joy to experience the one moment we are in, without whirling thoughts of yesterdays and fearful projections of tomorrow? It might be difficult even to imagine a now that is complete with everything that we need . . . a peaceful now . . . a joyous now!

Hanh also said that: *"Mindfulness is the miracle which can call back in a flash one dispersed mind and restore it to wholeness so that we can live each moment of life."*

Many of us do not even know that we rarely live in the present moment. We were full of alcohol or drugs or both for so long that we can barely recognize reality. And often when we do, we are afraid of it. We often feel it is not in our control. We want to tune out, escape, be someplace else or even somebody else. We certainly do not want to face whatever it is at the moment. It might be uncomfortable and we do not like being uncomfortable.

Learning to Take Control of our Reality

As you begin to meditate on a regular basis you will begin to notice miracles in your life. But this cannot happen regularly if you only meditate once in a while. If you meditate just once in a while, you might only notice miracles once in a while. It is really up to you how soon you want to feel better and how often you want to experience miracles!

"If the practitioner knows his own mind clearly, he will obtain results with little effort. But if he doesn't know anything about his own mind, all of his effort will be wasted."

Thuong Chieu,
Zen Master

You are now learning to use meditation not only as a tool for relaxation, but as a powerful tool for change, a positive tool for healthy change.

"Came to believe that a power greater than ourselves can restore us to sanity."

Step 2
Twelve Steps and Twelve Traditions

As you train your mind more and more in your sitting meditation, you will gradually be able to bring this same quiet and awareness to all other areas of your life. You will begin to hear your *self-talk* more and more.

Turn the Thought Over!

You will become aware that the negative tapes that you are playing are not from today but from yesterday. And by listening to them with a very gentle, nonjudgmental mind, you will be able to isolate each negative thought and make a conscious decision not to let it affect you, not to let it be a barrier to your growth any longer.

It is very helpful to begin to write down what you hear. Begin to keep a notebook with you. This is very helpful in putting a light on your stumbling blocks, your negative tapes.

old tapes can keep us from growing

Listen. Do not judge! Just accept that you have played a negative tape. Do not struggle against it or beat yourself in any way. Put no energy at all into the tape or it will continue to have power over you.

Write "it" down and then look at it.

Accept "it" as a stumbling block. Be grateful for this learning experience!

Turn "it" over! See how you can convert it into a positive statement, a positive affirmation.

For example, if you were planning to apply for a new job and you heard your *self-talk say,* "You never do anything right!", after doing something wrong, *turn "it" over* to:

"It's perfectly OK to make a mistake."

Yes . . . *Turn the thought over to its flip side!*

Remember your dark room?

Remember that you must see first what you are bumping into before you can stop getting hurt. You must:

First put a light on in your dark room so that you can move the furniture instead of bumping into it. You must empty the room before it can be refurnished! You've come to a fork on your spiritual path.

Your Affirmation

"I am beginning to learn who I really am right now without judgment and with love and acceptance."

letting go of old negative
self-talk (tapes) and
filling in the space with
peace, love and goodness!

14

Fork In The Road

*"Most people fail because they do not wake
and see when they stand at the fork in the road
and have to decide."*

Erich Fromm

*"If you want greater prosperity in your life,
start forming a vacuum to receive it!"*

Catherine Ponder

Know that you are at a very important point at your life
right now. Know that you are on the verge of making a very
important discovery. This is your opportunity to make choices
and take responsibility for the quality of your life. Are you
ready for this? I think so or you wouldn't have come this
far.

You will soon see that everything that you tell yourself
that is negative keeps you from achieving your goals. These
are *old negative tapes*. They are from the past and have
nothing to do with this moment. They come from memories
of feelings and words and actions from other people and other
times.

It might be what you tell yourself today, but it did not come from you originally. Or if it did, it came from an experience in the past and still has nothing to do with the now.

You will get in touch with the blocks that keep you from achieving your highest good. These are based on negative beliefs and attitudes which keep you from seeing positive and loving things about yourself.

Your Affirmation

"I know that I am at choice today and I am willing to give up all the negative tapes that block me from growth and fulfillment."

15

Stumbling Blocks Into Stepping Stones

"The happiness of solitude is not found in retreats. It may be had even in busy centers. Happiness is not to be sought in solitude or in busy centers. It is in the self."

Sri Ramana Maharshi

One night when I was 38 years old and had been sober about a year, I went to visit my mother for supper. I went into the kitchen to help her serve and came out with a bowl of soup.

"Here", she said. "Let me help you with that so you won't spill it."

It was as if time stood still. Everything inside of me stopped. What I heard was years and years of "you're clumsy; you're careless; you're lazy; you're thoughtless; you can't do anything right." And my mother probably never even said any of those words directly to me. But that was what her *tone* meant to me, my interpretation of her *tone!*

And my "interpretation of her tone" kept me from doing many things in my life that might have "spilled the soup on the rug". I concluded that I was not worthy or good enough to . . . whatever.

And the beautiful thing that happened to me at that moment, with absolute clarity, was that *I knew I probably would not spill the soup*. And even if I did, *it would be all right*.

With that incident I had been given the gift of a beam of light on my dim path.

Here are some other negative tapes that might sound familiar to you:

"I'm not pretty enough."

"I'm not smart enough."

"If you really knew me, you wouldn't like me."

"I'll probably make a fool of myself."

"What will the neighbors think!?"

"It's too dangerous . . . I might get hurt."

And on and on and on. We hold ourselves back. We don't take chances. We stay the victim of our negative tapes.

Not until we see this will we find the power to change.

Our true feelings have been blocked by:

1. **Addictions.** Whatever we chose as a mechanism to escape from reality.
2. **Denial.**
3. **Fear.** Which stays in the way of seeing our true selves.

These have been the hindrances to our freedom, just as our character defects keep us making the same mistakes over and over again until we are willing to look at them in clear light.

Some meditations stop the mind from thinking. This was my experience with TM. Insight Meditation, on the other hand, brings clarity to the mind. It allows us to watch what is going on without reacting to negative tapes and impulses.

> *"Stopping the mind does not bring wisdom, what brings wisdom is understanding the nature of the mind . . .*
>
> *"Mindfulness is the most powerful means of cutting through the hindrances. We can sit with any of them and rather than blocking our meditation, they can become the object of the investigation."*
>
> *Steven Levine*

Your Affirmation

"Today I have the courage to look without fear at what needs to be changed in my life."

16

Recipe For Change

"On the day you cease to change you cease to live."

Anthony de Mello

Our path to recovery has been overwhelmed by our obsession with the past and our worry for the future. We have ignored the Now . . . this living moment. The greater the hold of the Past in our lives, the greater is our fear of the Future . . . and the less we experience our Now.

As the power of the Past is lessened, our fear of the Future diminishes . . . and our Now begins to give us Joy!

In direct proportion to our increase in our ability to experience our Now, our experience of Love and Peace and Serenity increases, which is really what we have been looking for all our lives.

1. **Meditation**
   Quiet and clear the mind

2. **Hearing Your "Self-talk"**
   Hearing your negative tapes
   Begin to see what is between you and your higher power
   Begin to be able to hear God's will for you
   Discover "it"
   Uncover "it"

3. **Acceptance**
   Stop the denial
   See "it"
   Own "it"
   Live with "it"
   Become friends with "it"
   Let "it" lose its power!

4. **Forgiveness (Empty)**
   Shining the light on "it"
   Seeing "it" as a stumbling block
   Be willing to let "it" go
   Forgive yourself and anyone else involved

5. **Visualize (Fill)**
   Picture yourself without "it" (not the incident but the feelings)
   How do you feel?
   What are the good feelings?

6. **Energize**
   Unblock your natural power
   Feel the power of your inner guide
   Feel the power of the universe
   Begin to trust your inner voice

7. **Symbolize (Fill)**
   Create a quick symbol to bring up
   Every time the old feelings return

8. **Affirm (Fill and Energize)** . . .

I prefer to feel peace and love instead of anger and guilt.

My past no longer owns me.

I am free of old, negative feelings.

I forgive myself and all others today.

I am one with my Higher Power and the Universe today.

I no longer give power to the conversations that go on in my head.

The important things to remember about affirmations are that . . .

- They are stated in the present tense, in the *now*.
- They are positive.
- You act and feel as if they are true.
- You repeat them verbally or in writing (or both) at least 10 times a day for 21 days.

You will begin to see changes in yourself within **three days!**
Stay with them for **seven days** and your life will be much better in the area that you are affirming!
In **21 days** you will not recognize yourself in that area!

Your Affirmation

"I am no longer the victim of my past nor do I fear my future."

17

Self-talk

*"Our own creative energy is waiting to move
through us once we get out of our own way.
Cleansing the mind of negative thought, quiet-
ing the chatter and becoming one with the
moment provides the environment for this
energy to flow through us."*

Ruth Ross

As you get further into the practice of meditation, you
will begin to notice more and more of what goes on inside
your head. You will soon become aware as you never have
before of the endless conversations, observations, judgments,
opinions and projections that constantly occur in your mind.
You will become aware the longer you allow this to happen
that you are not always comfortable with this endless activity,
that it was often this very unrest that sent you running away
before into your addiction.

Now by allowing yourself to experience your inner
conversations, your "self-talk", you will soon begin to know
yourself on a new level. You will be able to observe the way
you react, experience, feel and think. The longer you practice
and the more that you really listen, the more clearly you
will see who you really are.

You will begin to hear the "self-talk" that has influenced you throughout your entire life, without you even knowing it. You will finally begin to shine a light on the tapes that have come from old experiences, other people and other places and have absolutely no value in your life today.

And as you learn to meditate at a deeper level, you will begin to learn the sources of this "self-talk", you will learn how to change it into a positive factor in your life today. In the quiet of your meditation, you will learn to observe it at a detached level. The more that you can see and hear, the more you can accept. And as you gently accept the truth about yourself, old tapes will begin to lose their power over you. Their noise will gradually diminish. You will learn to take charge of your mind, and you will become free.

Staying With It
No Matter What

It is important to notice here how natural it is for you to want to run away or escape. Every time you have given in to this urge in the past, you have buried your truth more deeply. Stay with it, be with it, go through it and learn from it, no matter what.

At times your *self-talk* might become painful. *Self-talk* has been taped from old messages. As you begin to isolate old tapes, and this is a very important point for you to understand, you will become clearer about your conscious mind's conversations with itself. You might hear messages like the following:

"You're not good enough!"

"You'll never amount to anything!"

"Hurry up! There's more to do."

"There will never be enough for all of us."

"I'll never get what I need."

"Why bother? There will be smarter and more experienced people applying."

When you begin to hear that these are the messages that have blocked you from moving forward in many areas of your life, when you start to see that these messages and many like them came from times you might not like to remember in your past, your first impulse might be never to meditate again!

And the more painful the messages and memories are, the more desire you will have to relieve that pain. But remember, truth has always been blocked by your escaping into your addiction before. Just one drink or one pill or one bite won't help. Hiding is no longer an option if you want to live.

The Truth Is Not Gone Because Your Eyes Are Closed

But more often than not, self-talk is not painful, but fascinating! As you begin to hear the constant chatter that takes place in your mind, you will begin to understand many things. One will be the way you fail to hear all of the things other people say to you. You might notice that while someone else is talking, you are planning ahead to what you are going to say. Or your eye might have been caught by something interesting, and your mind is off and running.

Our minds are constantly chattering away, judging this, criticizing that, blaming this, praising that . . . commenting, commenting, commenting. Larry Rosenberg, a former meditation teacher of mine, described it as having a newscaster in our heads who is always explaining, describing, commenting! No wonder we are often exhausted!

My first understanding of this came when I began to practice Vipassana Meditation. For many years, probably all my life if I had been able to bring awareness to it, I would wake up very early in the morning, lie in bed and try to solve all my problems. I wouldn't only be trying to solve my problems for the day but I would go over and over and over all the problems and the plans that were lying before me. This could include all financial planning for my life along with how to pay today's bills. One morning as I was going through my regular routine of what I thought was "trying to figure it out", I suddenly became aware that all I was really doing was going over and over the same problems.

But how could I stop? I discovered a trick so simple I couldn't believe it worked. I did a modification of my meditation based on the concept that . . .

It is a proven fact that you cannot have two thoughts in your mind at the same time.

I began to breathe in *peace* with each in-breath. Sometimes I varied it with the word *love*. Very slowly I would

> Breathe in **peace**
> and breathe out
> *very gently.*
> Breathe in **peace**
> and breathe out
> *very gently.*

The next thing I knew it would be two hours later and I felt as if I had had the best sleep of my life!

This also works very well if you are having difficulty falling asleep. This is a very simple routine to do. If this doesn't work, there will be more exercises in the last part of this book.

Years later I read Dr. Herbert Benson's excellent book *Beyond The Relaxation Response*, where he refers to this phenomena as "loops" formed in the "wiring" of your brain and says that by focusing your thinking on word, sound, prayer or exercise, the chain of everyday worrisome thought is broken. He calls these mental patterns, these unproductive grooves or circuits that cause the mind to "play" over and over again, almost in voluntarily, the same anxieties or health-impairing thought "worry cycles".

Simply explained, these "worry cycles" create anxiety and stress. Meditation counteracts the harmful effects by relaxing our minds and our bodies.

The more meditation becomes a part of our daily lives, the more we become more aware of our *self-talk*. And we are going to hear what *blocks* us to growth and peace. We need to listen without being hard on ourselves. With our new awareness we will gain insight, and as we gain insight we will gain understanding and knowledge.

It is very important at this point to learn to be compassionate with ourselves. As we learn what really makes us tick and can come to love ourselves as we are, we will learn to accept and love others as they are, too. But this process must start with ourselves.

It is beautiful to experience being with ourselves at a level of complete acceptance. When that begins to happen, when you begin to give up resistance and needing to be perfect, a peace will come over you such as you have never known. When it is no longer important to always be right, you will begin to tune into others at a new level, at a new awareness. You will be able to really hear what other people are saying, and you will be able to accept their statements and beliefs. You will discover what it is like to be one with others and see that you are part of a larger universal picture. Your own space will begin to open and expand, and you will no longer have to be only with people who think like you and agree with you.

But how can you learn to listen and see with compassion? How can you learn to be gentle and understanding? It is time to bring *a gentle witness* into your life!

Your Affirmation

"It is so freeing to know that I am no longer
controlled by the voices that go on in my head."

18

Our Gentle Witness

"Keep the doors locked and we will be secure,"
says the ego.
Our heart responds, "But I'm not happy like that.
To which the ego replies, "Better safe than sorry."

Ram Dass
How Can I Help?

During infancy when we feel very powerless, we build survival mechanisms. When our needs are not being met, when we are afraid and hurt, we begin to build walls of self-protection and learn modes of behavior in order to get along.

This is the time that our image of ourself begins to develop. This is the time that the messages are formed that we are later to replay and replay at the "push of a button". We often refer to our reactions and say that someone has pushed our buttons. As we have seen, this is exactly the way it happens. When faced with a confrontation, early emotions long stored in our subconscious come up and we respond as we did to the earliest ones, not to today's event. We are not living in reality but on the fantasies and memories of our past.

"We feel powerless and vulnerable, and because these ideas are learned emotionally, before reason and perspective are fully operating, they may be suprisingly resistant to change as we grow older."

Ram Dass

We must find a way to detach, to not identify with our ego so that we may learn how to change and grow. If we are stuck with our solid views of ourselves, we will be committed to continually acting out the way we see ourselves.

We act like the persons we see ourselves to be.

We act in accordance with our self-image.

When the opinion changes, the performance follows.

Remember the meditation instructions which taught you to watch your thoughts? You also learned to watch your feelings and emotions and not to judge them. We must learn to accept what *is* before we can change anything.

While meditating, we watch our thoughts come in and pass on, our feelings come up and go away. The more we are detached from our thoughts and feelings, the more we learn that they are not permanent, that they come and they go, that they change. They do not remain the same. As we continue to do our sitting meditation we begin to experience this more and more. We are actually training our minds to continue this process throughout the entire day.

"To study the way is to study the self.
To study the self is to forget the self.
To forget the self is to be enlightened by all things.
To be enlightened by all things is to remove the barrier
between Self and Other."

Dogen Zenji

Buddha taught that the very basic roots of suffering came from resistance to unpleasant situations. We are either trying to hold on to something very tightly because we are afraid that we are going to lose it or we are trying desperately to get something that we do not have. He saw that we would always have pain in our lives but that was not our enemy. Our biggest enemy was our resistance to it.

As addicts and co-dependents we have resisted and hidden from pain all our lives. Not only have we run from pain, but from discomfort, fear, unpleasantness, restlessness, boredom, etc. You name it. If we didn't like it, we found a way not to feel it, a way not to look at it.

We never learned how to deal with any of this suffering except by running away. And if we didn't put something into our bodies to block our feeling or looked for another person or place to make it better, our mind would fantasize and rationalize so that we did not have to hear and face the truth.

Years into my own alcoholism I remember attending a play put on by my daughter's kindergarten class. The children were sweet and adorable, as only five-year-olds on their best behavior can be. They were all dressed up in their best clothes and smiles and singing *"What the World Needs Now is Love Sweet Love."* The sweetness and joy of their voices with the moving words of their song touched my heart so that it actually felt as if it were breaking, and I cried and cried. I remember, as clearly as if it were happening now, that I was aware that I had not truly felt joy and love in years. In that moment I knew I was alive. I knew what it was to feel alive. And it felt so good. I remember saying to myself that I used to feel like that often, and I knew then that most of the time I felt dead inside.

By blocking my pain with alcohol I had blocked my ability to love. My joy of living was buried under layers and layers of pain and self-pity and denial.

As we learn more and more to be in the now, we are going to be aware of discomfort, suffering and pain. But if we continue to block it, we cannot feel love. We cannot experience joy. We cannot become one with the universe.

So we need to find a way to come to know ourselves gently, without judgment, without displeasure. We need to find a way to examine all that happens within ourselves without fear. We need to look at our discomfort, agitation, restlessness, boredom and insecurities. We need to find a way to look at ourselves and accept ourselves just as we are. Only then will we learn to love ourselves and stop running away.

my
gentle witness

When we begin to watch ourselves, it is as if we have a second person watching our minds work. It is as if we have developed a Gentle Witness who does not get caught up in our soap operas, who does not become a news commentator, who does not judge us or our thoughts or our actions as right or wrong. This witness becomes like a best friend, someone who is always there and just *is* with us. A friend that notices and points out, but doesn't judge.

With this witness, this trusted companion, we can begin to trust ourselves. We begin to see ourselves and learn about ourselves.

I had an opportunity to experience this recently. I became a witness to my own Gentle Witness in action.

One day I became aware of myself in the middle of a frustrating experience and realized that I was handling it as I had always done in the past, feeling uncomfortable and anxious. I was frustrated, tense and fearful.

I wanted to secure an $8,000.00 line of credit with a leasing company, and I was told that the process would take 24 hours. At first I was relatively confident that we would get it. As the end of the 24 hours drew near I had not heard from the leasing company, my confidence began to diminish. Uncomfortable feelings began to surface. I became aware that I was feeling fear of rejection, and my mind began to project conversations and situations that had no basis in the reality of the moment. I was planning that I would go into the leasing company and demand that they change their minds. "What right did they have to refuse us?" I demanded in my mind indignantly.

I suddenly became aware that my body was agitated, my mind was racing and I was extremely upset. And then I really heard myself and saw my fear and decided that I had better try that which I had been teaching and writing about myself.

As this awareness took place I allowed myself to become gentle with myself. I began to talk to myself and tell myself that it was OK to be nervous, "Oh! Those are old feelings! You haven't had them for awhile! That's OK."

I gently brought my attention to my breathing and I began to breathe in and breathe out very slowly. I then began telling myself that the leasing company was now in the process of accepting us. I said this slowly over and over again, as I was very slowly and very consciously breathing in and breathing out. I called the leasing company but the person who was making this decision was out to lunch. I had other things to do, so I began doing some errands. Each time the old feelings of fear and rejection would come up in my stomach, I would return my concentration to my breathing and concentrate on the positive message that the leasing company was now in the process of accepting us. I watched myself watch myself and acknowledge and smile at just what I was doing, being pleased with the noticeable changes I kept on experiencing, and was even thinking to myself that I was glad that all this was happening so that I could write about it and share it with others.

When I returned to my office, I called again and was greeted cheerfully with, "You're all set. Your credit has been approved."

I am not saying that my positive thinking actually changed any decisions. What I did made me feel better. I was living in the *now*. I did not have to project failure. If we had been rejected, I then would have dealt with the feelings of rejection at the time that they were appropriate, only when they happened.

It is through practicing like this that we begin to become more gentle with ourselves. We slowly change negative tapes to positive ones, old habitual ways of doing things to newer, healthier ways. As we become more gentle with ourselves, we begin to love ourselves. And as we begin to love ourselves, we become more open and we are able to love others in a more richly satisfying manner.

We now move to the next step of our path . . .

1. *We quiet our minds through meditation.*
2. *We begin to gain insight into our minds.*
3. *We begin to accept so that we can change.*

There will be no denying that we will hear negative tapes. Negative tapes are one of our biggest blocks. And if we are to ever turn these tapes around, we have to first hear them, and then we have to own them. We have to accept them before we can do anything about them.

Your Affirmation

"I will be my own best friend today and treat myself gently, and with love and respect."

19

Negative Tapes

"The greatest discovery of any generation is that human beings can alter their lives by altering their attitudes of mind."

Albert Schweitzer

You have now come to a terrific place! Granted it might not feel good, but you are beginning to reach your truth. And as the old axiom goes:

"The truth will set you free!"

You are beginning to hear the negative tapes that have kept you from reaching your fullest potential. You are now seeing the stumbling blocks that have been your barriers to honest relationships, love and serenity. But most important, you are discovering what has covered your true inner feelings and has kept you from hearing your inner voice and thus connecting with God's will for you.

From the moment of birth we store all the messages that we receive. These messages come from words, touches, feelings, sensations and thoughts. They also come from our perspective of what is happening to us and around us.

Perspective is very important. For example, imagine two children are playing ball. Their team wins and they are elated and go home to tell their families their good news. One set of parents shows their pleasure for their child's success by praise and sharing the excitement. When the other child goes home, mother is passed out in the bedroom, the house is a mess and there is no one there to talk to or share the good news. The good feelings are soon lost in the pain of the situation and the game becomes a very small part of the memory.

Later, the experience would then be remembered totally differently by the two children. If asked about it, one would describe it with shining eyes, while the other might barely remember it. The game had become just another "so what" for the second child because her feelings of pain and abandonment were so much greater than her recollection of the event itself.

Another child is fed on time and goes to sleep in dry diapers after being held and cuddled. Next door the father did not come home on payday and the fuel was not delivered. The child in that house cries and cries but no one answers.

Encouragement or discouragement. Love or neglect. More of one side than the other? Never sure which? Confusion or peace. Support or abandonment. The list could go on for ever. I am sure you are getting the picture.

You Act Out
Who You Think You Are

Imagine your mind like a vast computer, a massive storage depot for all your memories and experiences. Every time you were told you were good and that you were loved, a positive button was pushed. Each time you had a negative experience or message, a negative button was pushed. These messages take up who you *think* you are. Notice the word *think*. You continue to repeat these same messages until you learn or experience different ones.

Each time you are in a new experience which reminds you of an old experience, the old buttons are pushed and you again act as you did in the past. You respond. You react. And your reactions often have little validity or relevance to what is happening today.

Put more simply, the past is stored in your subconscious automatically. In a similar experience, therefore, your subconscious responds and your conscious mind is fooled into thinking that the past is now.

For example, for many years I had a very difficult time with any kind of arguments. Only later in recovery did I learn that my discomfort was not necessarily caused by the immediate argument. Instead my entire body was responding to old fights with my father, who had a very bad temper at times. I was rarely spanked but the threat was always there. There had been a few times when he lost his temper and took off his belt to swing it at me. I remember running to my room and locking my door while he screamed at me from outside. My mother would tell me to open the door because she was afraid that my father would have a heart attack. His voice would get louder and louder and his face became redder and redder. If I opened the door, there would be the danger of getting a beating, and if I didn't open the door, I might be responsible for the death of my father!

No wonder my body and my mind reacted from these old experiences. Not until I was able to see this by putting a light on the past was I able to let it go and be more in the now.

Dr. Herbert Benson, in his book *Beyond the Relaxation Response*, has a wonderfully simple explanation of why we respond to today's situation with old tapes. He says that "the reality for our organs can be what the mind perceives as reality and then transmits in physical messages to them."

Imagine that there are billions of cells in the brain that are part of circuits that haven't been connected. They have to be wired. Every time we experience something new, wiring is put into place and we have learned this particular piece of knowledge. There is now a "new mentally created circuit or pathway."

These mental wires make up the network for what we know as our memories, and memories may intrude in disturbing and uninvited ways into our lives. When we experience something new, our brain remembers an old time. Our bodies do not know that it is an old time because the brain is experiencing it now. Benson says that as far as your body is concerned, what's going on in your mind during a dream is real, and a short dream may be enough to cause dramatic changes in your body. This can work to make you feel good as well as bad.

We quiet our minds through meditation
We begin to hear our self talk
We begin to see our negative tapes
We get in touch with our blocks that have
　　been keeping us stuck

What are our Blocks?

it's time to be rid of those blocks!

Imagine that you have been on a very long journey. In fact you have! You have traveled your entire life to get to this very moment. Imagine that each experience and feeling that you have had has been recorded on a computer disk. By now you will have built up quite a collection of computer disks, each one full of memories.

Our minds are very much like computers. We have a conscious and subconscious mind. We use our conscious mind approximately 10% of the time, while our subconscious mind is controlling us 90% of the time.

Some of these messages take the form of guilt and shame. Others come masked as a poor self-image. And yet others stay around as fear and resentments and anger, to mention a few.

Every experience that we have is recorded in our subconscious. It just stays there recorded. It does not do anything until it is called upon. Every thought that we have is recorded in our subconscious, too.

Our subconscious does not know the difference between real and imagined experiences. If you have been slapped as a child, that experience, the visual picture and the feelings that took place at the time, are recorded. If the same person threatened you again with punishment, your subconscious would remember those first feelings as if they had happened again, reinforcing your fear of that person.

Maybe you attended school on a day that you were not prepared to be called on and, of course, were called on. The embarrassment of not knowing the answer and thinking that everyone else in the room knew the answer created terrible feelings of dismay, stress, anxiety and guilt. Often the stress you felt was so great that the next time that you were called upon, you relived that incident in your subconscious mind and, even if you were prepared, memory of the old incident created stress in the new incident. You couldn't remember any of the answers.

Now we know that all of us are born with a spark of pure love within. And we have seen how the years of experiences, real and imagined, have covered this spark of energy and love.

But we are survivors. Anyone who has lived until this moment and is still alive and able to read this page is a survivor. In order to survive we have thought it necessary to protect ourselves from pain and unhappiness. We have done this with our drugs and alcohol, and we have done this by building defense mechanisms. We have done what we thought we had to do so that we wouldn't feel that dreadful pain of rejection and disappointment.

So we have built walls with such self-talk as . . .

"I don't care if I'm not invited."

"I'd rather be alone anyway."

"No one will ever understand me."

"I'll never be smart enough to be successful."

"I have a terrible memory."

We have produced these tapes for ourselves at a subconscious level. Usually we did not even know when we created them. Often they have originated in what someone else said to us, such as a parent telling us that we were no good. We hear what they think of us, their image of us, and we take it on as truth for our own self-image. If we do not feel as good as everyone else, of course, we would rather stay home from a party. We have experienced embarrassment and rejection in the past and think that if we go to another party, we will just repeat the same unpleasant experience. Of course, we think that we are happier alone.

Along with these pictures of unpleasant memories we have carried the pain of the unpleasant experiences as well. We have continued to feel angry and resentful at some people from our past. We have to be willing to let these go.

Very often our self-esteem is very low but we are so used to thinking in a negative way about ourselves that we are not even aware that we are blocking our own progress.

Your Affirmation

"Negative tapes are from yesterday and have
no rightful place in my today!"

20

Low Self-Esteem

"Nothing has changed but my attitude.
Everything has changed."

Anthony de Mello

We Act Out
Who We Think We Are

If we have low self-esteem, we are going to act as if we are unworthy of good relationships, rewarding jobs, success and happiness. If we think we don't deserve good things to happen to us, we will be sure to see that they don't. We will either not go for something good, or we will sabotage anything good that comes along.

Know that we do not do this at a conscious level. As you have learned, we are still acting out old tapes from early childhood and we will continue to do so until we know how to change them.

Father Leo Booth, in his book *"Spirituality and Recovery"* says: "If we have a poor opinion of ourselves, if we do not think we are of much value, if we are unable to see any features in our lives, then it is not surprising we are destroying ourselves."

The images we have of ourselves prepare us for either success or failure. We act out our images and opinions of ourselves. And very often, the opinion we have of ourselves is not even our own. It came from our parents or our teachers or someone else who was influential to us early in our formative years.

> *"Much of what we know, both intuitively and rationally, is layered over by decades of learning to doubt ourselves (women) and giving over much of our decision-making and creation-making power to others. By meditating, we can go past these conditioned layers of self-doubt and discover our own wisdom."*   Hallie Iglehart

All our negative past experiences block us from having energy today. We are stuck. We can't move forward until we become unblocked. But just knowing this isn't enough.

So again we are going to listen to our *self-talk*. We are going to hear our negative tapes. And as we listen to the very tapes that keep us in a state of low self-esteem, we are going to *shine a light* on them, *accept* them as *blocks* and, *visualize* the new way we want to be.

Fear is one of the factors holding us back. *Fear* keeps us from changing. *Fear* often keeps us from looking deeper within so that we could put a light on our stumbling blocks.

Unwillingness to forgive is another factor holding us back. If we are not willing to forgive ourselves and others, we are stuck in the past. We are stuck in old feelings of anger and resentment and self-pity and cannot experience the now.

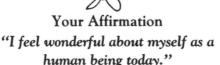

Your Affirmation
*"I feel wonderful about myself as a
human being today."*

21

Forgiveness

"Forgiveness is an inner correction that lightens the heart. It is for our peace of mind first. Being at peace we will have peace to give others, and this is the most permanent and valuable gift we can possibly give . . .

"The root of the word forgive is to let go. Forgiveness is a relinquishing of an unwelcome train of thought . . .

"Forgiveness is a gentle refusal to defend ourselves against love any longer. It is a willingness to perceive everyone, including ourselves, as either expressing love or feeling a need for love.

"Any form of attack is a call for help, and the answer to every call for help is gentleness."

Gerald G. Jampolsky
Love is Letting Go of Fear

Full recovery is impossible without forgiveness. Peace of mind is impossible without forgiveness. A point will come where further growth is impossible without forgiveness.

Lack of forgiveness presents us with roadblocks which hold us back and keep us stuck in misery. Some of the things that we insist on holding on to when we refuse to forgive are . . .

Anger	Fear
Resentments	Guilt
Being Right	Shame
Staying Still	Hate
Blame	Getting Even
Being-A-Victim	Dependencies

The list could go on and on.

Resentments keep us in the past. We cannot be in the now when we resent. When we resent, we experience the old feelings over and over again. As has already been explained, our bodies do not know the difference between a real experience and thoughts. If you are re-feeling, reliving a past experience in your mind, your body responds as if the act were happening right now. So when you remember something that you are angry about, the feelings of anger replay throughout your body doing damage to it.

The root of the word *forgive* is to *let go*.

Even when we know how damaging holding on is, why is it so hard to let go?

Until we know that we benefit from forgiving, we will never want to give up the agenda to which we are holding so tightly. Until we know that we forgive so that we can feel better for our own peace of mind, we will continue to hang on to resentments and be miserable.

At any given time we are actually holding on to what is only a memory of an event that happened in the past. It is no longer real in the now. It is only a memory that we have in our minds and therefore re-feel in our bodies and emotions.

Imagine yourself in a very good frame of mind. Now imagine someone who has made statements that have caused you pain. Let yourself feel your feelings about those statements. Now imagine that this person has just come into your room. This person does not say a word but merely looks at you. You no longer feel good. Instead you remember the other times that you have felt pain. Without anything new happening, you have given this person the power to take away all your good feelings.

Another word for forgiveness is *atonement*. A *Course of Miracles* talks about atonement as At-One-Ment or becoming one with the other person. Atonement is a correction of our belief of separation. We become *at one* by becoming willing to give up that which separates us. We become *at one* when we know that we are both children of the universe with the same purpose deep within. We feel at peace when we discover our similarities, rather than our differences.

Forgiveness Is A Choice

"How do you know whether to choose the stairs to heaven or the way to hell? Quite easily. How do you feel? Is peace in your awareness? Are you certain which way to go? . . . If not you walk alone."

A Course in Miracles

I sometimes find it very helpful to picture the other person with a heart inside their body in the shape of a valentine heart. And then I picture a similar heart within me. I can finally overlook the events that have happened that are standing between us. I can see then that the events are only memories in my mind which I can choose to let go of, and no longer exist in reality.

"A cloud does not put out the sun."

No matter what we are thinking and feeling our suffering and resentments do not change the fact that somewhere within the other person, however deeply buried it might be, they also have a spark of love and life. Our unwillingness to forgive is all that is standing in the way of our seeing it.

A *Course in Miracles* teaches that every act is an expression of love or a cry for help. A miracle is a shift in perception, a change in our awareness. When we know that we have experienced a miracle, we suddenly see things differently.

The More That We Can Become Empty, The More Room We Make To Be Filled.

When we become willing to let go of our resentments, we will open up to love. We experience At-One-Ment. As we are willing to have these blocks removed, letting ourselves be emptied of that which has kept us strangers from our fellow human beings for so long, we will begin to let love in and experience the miracle of forgiveness again and again.

As we become filled with love and really begin to experience our sameness, our worlds will get bigger and bigger. No longer will we be confined within the barriers and limitations of our past. Where we once needed a small circle of friends with similar personalities from the same background, we now become more and more open to finding love and goodness in everyone.

Your Affirmation

*"Today I choose to let go of all barriers that
block me from seeing the love and goodness
in myself and others."*

"the more that we
can become empty, the
more room we make to
be filled."

22

Special Symbols

"What we expect, believe and picture, we usually get."

Ruth Ross

When you take time to do your regular daily meditations, you can use the process in Chapter 5 to bring relaxation through your entire body and quieten your mind.

There will be other times when you will want to go into your special place or just relax so that you can do visualizations and affirmations without meditating first. It will be necessary to feel relaxed so that these exercises can be as effective as possible.

Once you get used to the process of meditation, it will become easier and easier to relax at will. For example, if you are standing in line in the bank or late for an appointment, and feel yourself getting irritated and uptight at the apparent powerlessness of the situation, you can bring your attention to your breathing and relax. As you bring your attention to your breath as it goes in and goes out of your nose, you can feel peace and relaxation flow through your entire body. You get in a new habit of responding with relaxation when you bring your attention to your breath.

Another way of relaxing at will is to visualize a symbol that means relaxation to you. For example, a gently soaring seagull flying high in the sky, or a sailboat drifting on the distant horizon. One person I know uses a waterfall.

Find a symbol that makes you feel peaceful.

*Close your eyes and let yourself picture
   that symbol.
Let peace and relaxation flow through your
   entire body.
Feel the peace.
Know the peace.
Enjoy the peace.*

Keep this symbol for as long as you want it. Change it or vary it whenever you wish. The main point is that it will take you to a state of relaxation that works for you.

Your Affirmation

*"Peace and relaxation flow through me
with every breath that I take."*

23

NUTS!
Are You Ready To Say
Nuts To The Old Ways?

*"Healing is accomplished the instant the
sufferer no longer sees any value to pain."*

A Course of Miracles

A Fun Way To End
Negative Thinking

Negative thinking is so often a part of our minds that
we rarely notice anything wrong with it. We just take it for
granted that that's the way we are. We let negative tapes
perpetuate our negativity, such as . . . "I'm too old to
change", or "You can't teach an old dog new tricks!"

But now that we have learned to:

Meditate — to quiet our minds

Listen — to our *Self-Talk*
Accept — the truth about ourselves
and
Become willing to change

We can no longer accept our negativity as a way of life! We are ready to be good to ourselves and put all this work into action.

Remember . . .
You can only have one thought in your mind at
    a time.
You can choose whether that thought is positive
    or negative.

The more times we turn a negative thought into a positive one, the more the deep grooves of the negative tape will wear out and the positive tape will begin to fill in and take its place. In time positive tapes will begin to become the new habit and we will be giving ourselves new messages and getting positive results.

Are you really ready for change? If so, you are now at the point where it is happening.

Each time you hear your *self-talk* being a negative barrier to your growth, yell *stop!*

Picture a large red stop sign, with big, black letters that spells *stop!*

And then say to yourself *nuts!*

NUTS stands for *Negative* and *Unpleasant Thought-Stopping*

Now it is difficult to picture a Stop Sign in your mind and yell *stop* at yourself without smiling. But it is even more difficult to say *NUTS* to yourself without smiling.

So remember this little trick. It works!

Your Affirmation

*"I am putting a large stop to
all my negative self talk today!"*

24

Going Home

". . . As long as we stand outside, we are outsiders."

D. T. Suzuki

There is a very special place inside each and everyone of us. It is a place where we are perfectly safe, a place where we find peace. It is where the very core of existence lies, where our truth lives. It's that special place we talked about earlier that has been buried throughout the years where our spark of energy and life and love lives.

Over all these years our need to fulfill our longings and desires has caused us to reach outward rather than inward. As we took more and more of what was out there, we found that it helped us less and less, and we became addicts or co-dependents or both.

It was very natural that if we felt "less than", we would want to fill up with "more" to feel better. But the process of filling up cannot happen until we first empty. And we cannot empty until we see what has to be emptied. And we cannot see what has to be emptied until we put a light on in our dark room.

Using Your Recipe

1. Bring quiet to your mind
2. Begin to know yourself by using all your senses

Meditation is your tool to look within. Meditation is your tool to quiet your mind long enough to begin to put a light on in your dark room. Meditation is your tool to quiet your mind to begin your journey home to self-awareness and self-knowledge and wisdom.

You are now ready to start this special journey within. Know that you are not alone and that you will soon know that you never have to be alone again. You are being led by a power greater than yourself. As you open more and more to the energies of the universe, you will find your inner self or true self.

You will go home to your very source. This path to your source has to be traveled so that you can be in the here and now.

You will not be sorry! It is what you have waited for and looked for all your life. All the time that you have been reaching out, your answers were within you. All the time that you were trying this or that, here or there, this person or that person, your answers for peace and serenity were no further away than your own breath.

Special Meditation to go into your inner sanctuary

Get yourself into a comfortable position. Begin to relax. Close your eyes gently and begin to bring your attention to your breathing. Bring to mind your relaxation symbol. Now spend a few minutes following your meditation routine.

Take some time to think about how you would design a perfect place for yourself. It can be anywhere and made out of anything. It can be inside or out of doors, made of any material that you choose, and of any design that makes you happy.

Create a place where you are perfectly safe, where you feel really good about yourself. Know that nothing can happen to you in this place that you do not want to have happen. This is your place . . . just for you. No one else can enter it unless you invite them.

As you begin to feel relaxed let yourself go deep within.

Let yourself go deep within . . .

 to this very special, quiet place inside.

  Let yourself go . . .

   deep within . . .

    to your very special place . . .

   where you are completely safe.

This is your special place . . . your inner sanctuary.

Take some time to use all your senses to know your place. Are there any special sounds? Any special aromas? How does it feel beneath your fingers and beneath your feet? What time of year is it? What time of day? Is it warm or cold?

Know that you can come here any time you wish. Know that you can change it any time you wish . . . add to it . . . change the scenery . . . the furniture . . . the time of year . . . the time of day.

Know that this is your special, safe place where you can be alone to learn about yourself and find peace.

Your Affirmation

"It feels so safe to know that there is always a special place within me where I can feel peace."

25

Finding Our Inner Guide

*"As we open the connections
between the conscious and the
subconscious aspects of our
beings, we reclaim our
spiritual selves
from isolation and neurosis."*

Hallie Iglehart

*inside your special place
lives an inner guide.*

You are now in the process of removing the negative,
destructive messages that have been holding you back and
keeping you stuck. You are beginning to see that you did
not create these tapes. They really originated from others
in your early life, and you have taken them on as your own.
The more you meditate, the more this new awareness
deepens. As you get farther into your reprogramming process
and begin to change negative tapes to positive ones, where

are you going to get your answers? Who will give you your truth? If your past tapes no longer work for you, where do you go from here?

Deep within all of us lives our own truth at a level that we have rarely been able to trust consistently. Now that you know that you have a special place within you where you can always go and feel safe and find peace, special answers will soon be yours.

Deep within you, at that very special place where your spark of life is beginning to twinkle and shine again, lies your inner knowledge at a very gut level. Call it intuition . . . inner knowing . . . gut knowing. Whatever you want to call it, it is yours and you are the only one who can find it.

Inside your special place lives an Inner Guide, who can be called your Inner God or Goddess, a Special Friend, a Sponsor or any other name that makes you feel comfortable. I call mine my Inner Goddess. For the sake of ease I will refer to her as an Inner Goddess from now on. You can just substitute your own name whenever you choose.

Your Inner Goddess has always been there. You just covered her up every time you were hurt and disappointed. Every time you had an unpleasant experience you covered her with layer after layer of blocks. Each time you saw your parents fighting . . . each time you were abused or attacked or put down or abandoned . . . you put on another layer. You become less and less able to feel your emotions and less and less able to trust yourself. Every time you turned to a drink or a drug or another dependency or escape, she hid deeper within you and further away from your reach.

You have buried your Inner Goddess, and it is time to set her free. It is time to give rebirth to sleeping parts of yourself long buried in fear, guilt, frozen anger, resentments, memories, alcohol, drugs and other dependencies. It's time to find your own truth!

Special Meditation
To Find Your Inner Guide

Let yourself relax. Begin to get ready to go to your special place inside . . . your inner sanctuary, so that you can meet your inner guide.

Take all the time you need to get comfortable. Let yourself feel your relaxation symbol. Begin to bring your full attention to your breath. Let your mind slowly settle down and be quiet.

Quietly
slowly
go down
to your special place.

Bring in good feelings about yourself.

Let yourself know that you are safe and that this is a place where only good can happen. Let your entire body feel at peace.

Now let yourself be out of doors. Take time to look around and feel what the weather is with your entire body. Look up at the sky and see if it is clear or cloudy. Maybe there are just a few clouds that are drifting by. Feel the time of day and the time of year. Do you hear any birds or animals? Is there a special scent of grass or flowers? Feel the ground beneath your feet. Bend down and touch the earth with your fingers. Pick up some soil and let it run through your fingers and fall back to earth. Hear the sound as it hits the ground.

Look up and see a winding path before you. The path goes as far as your eye can see and ends at the top of a hill. Know that someone is walking slowly towards you on the other side of the hill. Very gradually a head is beginning to appear and then an entire body. Begin to walk toward that person. See if you can see what she is wearing and what she looks like. Can you make out the features on her face?

When you get close enough, reach out your hand in

welcome. Walk slowly back with her to your special place. Be welcoming and thank her for coming to you. Ask her if she has a name. Tell her yours.

When you get inside your special place, take time to show her around and make her comfortable. Sit across from her and look directly into her eyes. Ask her if she has a special message for you.

Share where you are in your life and tell her about a problem you are now having. Ask her if she has any advice or answers for you.

If you don't hear any answers, do not be concerned. This will come in time. Just sit there quietly. Be with each other. It is fine if you do not hear words or even if you don't see her. Just know that she is there. In time all this will become clearer and clearer.

Whenever you feel ready, say 'goodbye' and thank her for being there.

Know that you can bring her back any time you want. Know that you can share anything with her and it will be safe. You can trust her completely.

Stay with your good feelings for a while.

Get ready to bring these good feelings of trust back with you.

Know that you never have to be alone again.

Very gradually get ready to come back to your room. Be sure you count to five before you open your eyes.

Your Affirmation

"I am learning to trust my own inner truth today."

26

Wish List

*"Our ability to want is a magical gift. When we
are excited and motivated to want, we are experiencing a sense of aliveness, an inner awareness of
unlimited opportunities about us."*

Ruth Ross

Beginning to Turn "It" Around

This is an excellent exercise for shining light on your
negative tapes. Spend a few minutes with it. The result can
be a turning point in your recovery.

Gently close your eyes for a few moments.

Relax and be comfortable.

Gradually let your mind go through your entire body and
bring relaxation to each part of it.

Let your mind take you to your special sanctuary, your
special place. Go to your special place where you are safe
and happy, where nothing can harm you in any way.

Let yourself feel what it is like to be there.

Feel the warmth. Feel the safety. Feel the comfort. Feel the happiness. Take a little time to just be there.

Now that you know that you are safe and relaxed in your special place, bring to your mind an image of something you would like to be. This could be anything such as a career, a relationship or an experience. Whatever comes up for you first. It could be your wish to look different or to act different or to be different.

Picture this new person doing whatever it is that you would like to do. Picture how it would feel to be doing this or that, just as this new person would. Imagine how you would feel. Picture what you would look like.

Be that person . . .

Be that person now . . .

In your mind.

Stay with her/him and be her/him for a while.

Now gradually come back to the room, and bring this image of the person you would like to be with you. Be here now with your eyes opening, gradually becoming aware of your body in this room with your special image.

Now take a sheet of paper and write down what it was you imaged. Stay with that image for a while and write down all you can think of that was with you in your mind.

Now turn the paper over and write down all the thoughts that come up for you as to why you can't become that special image.

Examining Our Blocks

You have . . .

- Thought about what you wanted do.
- Found the reasons that you tell yourselves you can't.
- Learned that these were old, negative tapes to which you could choose not to listen. But what's next?

Since we have been programmed in our past at a subconscious level to feel badly about ourselves, to feel unworthy, we will need to change at two levels. First, we need to see what our defects are and we will go into that in more depth later in this process.

But for a start we can begin to become aware of our negative tapes, through exercises like these, and by just bringing awareness to our everyday lives through sitting and walking meditation, bringing awareness to our *now*.

By shining the light on our *now*, we will see, we will hear, we will feel, we will notice. And once we begin this process, we can never be the same again.

Your Affirmation

"I deserve wonderful things to happen in my life today!"

27

When Meditation Doesn't Seem To Be Going Well

"The less you expect, the less you judge, the less you cling to this or that experience as significant, the further you will progress. For what you're seeking is a transformation of your being far beyond that which any specific experience can give you. It is important to expect nothing, to take every experience, including the negative ones, as merely steps on the path, and to proceed."

Ram Dass

Sometimes we suddenly seem to come to a dead stop in our progress. We might think we are doing everything the same, but something is changing. This is usually a place for new answers. A time for patience.

This happened to me suddenly after being on a high from everything I was learning and experiencing in the early months of this new meditation. I couldn't wait to share what

I was learning with anyone and everyone who would listen to me. Then suddenly the joy seemed to leave me, and I felt as if I were no different than before.

I stayed with it, day after day, waiting for the good feelings to return. And then I saw that I was *not satisfied with the now* again. I was looking out there for it to get better. I wanted what I didn't have and *therefore was unhappy.*

I saw that I had also been using the harsh and judgmental yardstick of materialism to measure my success and failure, rather than the soft and gentle loving scales of spirituality.

At first, and only by looking back could I see this, I was meditating to seek God's answer so that I could live more successfully and stop my pattern of struggle. I was rushing into meditation as I had rushed into everything else in my life . . . sure it would succeed to give me what I wanted. I thought that the results of successful meditation would be that I would feel only good, and that my life around me would go as I wanted it to go. What I wanted was success as measured by my standards, but I did not know that then.

I began to feel very little peace . . . only turmoil and self-doubt and self-pity. I could feel very little love, and I knew I was getting smaller and darker alone. And the fears began to creep in again because I had left so much open space for them. The space that had been filled with love and light had become empty again and fear had plenty of room to return to its old, familiar home.

But I kept reading and I kept praying and I kept meditating. For I knew that although there were many blocks before me, I knew deep within I was on the right path.

And then I read:

"For He Would Make The Crooked Places Straight" . . .

And my heart said

Yes!

"For He *would* make the crooked places straight"!

And I still read and learned and saw that I had been demanding answers, and those answers I thought would be in successes. I had been facing in the wrong direction all along.

I had to get through layers and layers of questions to find the answer. I needed only to seek God and the rest would follow. I needed only to be still long enough to feel God in my life. I needed only to be quiet and breathe and open myself up to hear and feel and know a Power greater than myself in my life.

And only then did I feel peace.

I felt gentleness unfold in me and I felt soft. I felt all the harsh lines and angles that had been my body become gentle and soft again. And I knew I was a warm and loving person for I had stopped judging myself. I was just a child of the universe. I was love.

And that was enough because it was everything.

Only by going through our struggles and by sharing them with others so that they can see our victory over them by the power of God in our lives . . . do we become a light for others to follow.

> "Her step is light
> and as she lifts her foot to stride ahead
> A star is left behind,
> to point the way to those who follow her."

" i learned these things
new about me."

I had been going on the wrong path
    to change from struggle.
In my struggle to lose struggle,
    I struggled to find God!
I struggled to meditate,
    to read and to learn.
And nothing changed.
I still struggled.
I was pushing hard to find,
    rather than waiting quietly to hear.

I was racing to get "there" fast
    rather than slowing down to learn that
God was "here" all along . . .
    . . . deep within me.
I just had to quiet myself long enough
    to feel God's presence
    and know God was there.
It is the God within that we are
    quieting ourselves to hear.
We are learning to stop
    the constant chatter of our minds to
"Be still and know that I am God."

Your Affirmation

*"Even in moments of doubt I know that my
Higher Power is guiding me on my path today."*

28

"Busy Folks" Who Think They Have No Time To Meditate:

Take Five!

"For there is . . .time . . . for every purpose."
Ecclesiastes

For the days when you are racing with both your head and with your body, take just five minutes to read this meditation. When you are going full steam ahead and wonder why you are always busy, when you haven't one moment for yourself and wonder how you will ever get through your list of things you *must* do, when you wonder if you will ever have time to stop with friends or smell a rose, take five minutes to experience miracles.

Repeat the following words . . . slowly . . . taking at least five minutes to finish this exercise. Notice the changes occurring in you physically and mentally while you are reading this. (This particular meditation works even better if you can stop long enough to find a friend or a lover or a spouse to read it to you.)

Now just close your eyes for a few minutes and picture a clock. Design this clock out of any material you wish, with a special decoration just for you. Set the hands of the clock for five minutes from now. Know that you have time to take five minutes and feel good about yourself for doing it. Now open your eyes if you are doing this alone and read the following slowly, or just listen carefully if it is being read to you . . .

I have all the time that I need in the
   universe
      Today.
I have all the time and the energy that I need
      Today.
I have all the time and the energy and the
   direction that I need
      Today.
to do all that God wants me to do with my
   life
      Today.
My struggling is over.
I have turned over all my rushing to my Higher
   Power and it is out of my hands
      Today.
I am very slowly and
   very gently
      going to go on with my day,
Grateful that a Power greater than myself
   is supplying me with all that I need
      to do all that is good and right in my
         life . . .
            Today!
            Thank You!

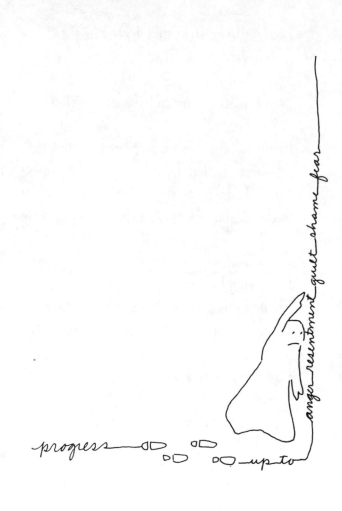

progress — up to

anger resentment guilt shame fear

29

Having A Hard Time Meditating

*"I don't think we should postpone meditation
until we move or clean the garage."*

Eknath Easwaran

Meditating Even When Your Self-talk Says:
"You don't want to meditate." or
"You don't have time to meditate." or
"Meditating isn't working."
. . . or even,
"I don't know what's wrong with me but I
just can't seem to meditate."

Over and over again I hear these words from people who
have at one time or other meditated with great results. I
have struggled to figure out how to help them, how to make
it easier for them. I finally concluded that I can't really do
that. That they, (and you, if and when you find yourself

in this position) must find a way to bring discipline into your life and meditate even when you don't want to.

> *"No one succeeds without effort. Mind control*
> *is your birthright. Those who succeed owe*
> *their success to their perseverance."*

> Sri Ramana Maharshi

Why is it that we don't always do what is best for us? Why do we put off completing things that we know we will feel good about when we are finished? Perhaps it is as simple as procrastination or laziness. Perhaps we just want what we want when we want it, and we would rather be doing something else at the time. Maybe it doesn't give us immediate gratification and we think that sleeping an extra twenty minutes would "feel better".

Rather than even trying to figure it out, bring logic to it or to psychoanalyze it, let's keep it really simple! Let's just say that it comes from a negative system that we don't want in our lives anymore. And with all that we have learned so far about changing our negative thought system by meditating, visualizing, acting "as if," and stopping our negative self-talk, just *know* that with a simple, painless and gentle plan, you can get back on the positive Path to Recovery and meditate without pain and struggle again!

Feel Like You
Are On A Detour?

If you can identify with this dilemma, know that just a few extra minutes of gentleness are needed. Don't beat yourself or judge yourself for this place that you are in. Know that it is quite common, that most of us have been there at some time or other and that if you use this as an opportunity to watch yourself and get to know yourself better in this kind of situation, great progress can be made. Use it as a stepping stone and not a stumbling block.

Know that all you need is a willingness or as we have said before, even a willingness to be willing. Here are a few suggestions that you can use to make this journey back easier.

"use it as a stepping stone and not a stumbling block!"

Watch yourself "not want to meditate" just as you watch a thought in meditation.

When the thought comes up that "I don't want to . . ." or "I can't" or "There is no time" or whatever, watch the thoughts as you would a cloud going by the sky. As you gently watch the thoughts without judging them, they become lighter and lighter until they pass by and disappear.

Watch them . . . just notice them and say "Oh, there I am again in this place. It's OK to be in this place."

Begin with a few affirmations to get you in the right frame of mind. Here are some suggested ones. Add others that will work for you.

"Today I am beginning my spiritual path to recovery."

"Nothing can stop me from growing today!"

"Today I am willing to meditate . . . whether I feel like it or not!"

"I'm Having A Hard Time!"

Visualization

Here is a visualization that will help you get up earlier in the morning. Do this right before going to bed so that it will be working on your subconscious while you are sleeping. You will not have to do anything at all but picture the scene and repeat the affirmations afterward.

Go very gently into your special place, your inner sanctuary. Find a wall or a flat surface and create a very beautiful clock. Design this clock out of any material you wish, with a special decoration just for you! Set the hands of the clock for twenty minutes earlier than you usually get up. Know that when you get up twenty minutes earlier tomorrow morning, you will do this without feeling deprivation. You will not be tired at all. In fact, you will wake up refreshed and looking forward to meditating!

Affirmation

Affirmations that have worked for others with this difficulty:

"*I am looking forward to meditating in the morning!*"

"*God is giving me all the strength and direction that I need to meditate regularly.*"

"*I meditate with joy and peace.*"

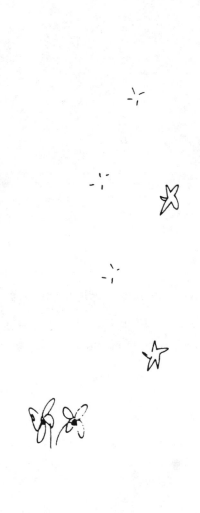

30

Visualizing For Change

*". . . thoughts of your mind have made you what you
are, and thoughts of your mind will make you
whatever you become from this day forward."*

Catherine Ponder

★ Meditation quiets our minds so we can see who we are.
★ Once we see who we are, we have to accept who we are.
★ Once we accept who we are, we can eliminate that which
is negative and destructive in our paths.
★ By emptying ourselves of the negative, we make space to
be filled with the positive.

Once we have become empty, we need to give ourselves
new messages so that we can act in new ways. Once the
old tapes are gone, visualization is an excellent tool with
which to reprogram the computers in our minds. Visualization
gives our bodies new messages. Our bodies believe what our
mind imagines.

"Creative visualization is magic in the truest and highest meaning of the word. It involves understanding and aligning yourself with the natural principles that govern the workings of the universe, and learning to use these principles in the most conscious and creative way."

Shakti Gawain

Everything New Begins In The Mind

Everything that is created begins in the mind. An author's imagination plans a book before it is written. An architect does the plans for a building mentally before putting them on paper. All pictures and plays and poems begin with a single thought.

Our minds are very powerful. What we see in our minds can affect the way our bodies feel.

Let's try a few examples:

Close your eyes very gently and picture a big lemon. Picture cutting the lemon in half with a knife. In your mind feel the sides of the lemon with your hands. Feel the rough surface. Now take that half of the lemon and put it in your mouth. Let yourself stay with that picture for a few minutes as your lips and tongue stay in contact with the lemon.

Now picture something else that you can drink or eat to take away the sour taste of the lemon. Put that in your mouth instead and feel the difference.

Some people cannot visualize pictures at first and have a stronger sense of knowing or feeling or smelling. Don't let this worry you if you can't actually see a picture. That will come with time and practice. In the meantime use any sense that is the strongest for you so that you can experience the visualizations.

Now picture that you are driving in a car. It is early evening and the road is empty and you have the music on the radio. You are very relaxed. Everything is peaceful! Suddenly a dog runs out from nowhere and is almost in front of your car. You slam on the brakes and swerve avoiding the dog by inches. You sit there for a few minutes, grateful that you missed the animal but conscious of all the feelings that went on in your body because of this near miss.

Thoughts tell our bodies how to respond.

It is now time for you to be in charge of those feelings. Visualizations are a way to change being controlled by old, negative feelings.

Remember, we act out who we think we are and we can feel physically what our minds tell us to feel.

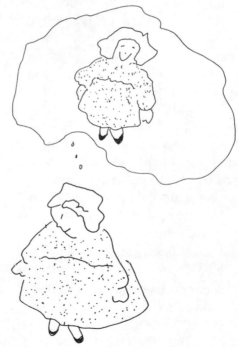

visualizations are like dress rehearsals!

Begin A List For Change

As you begin to listen to your *self-talk* and hear that which blocks you from becoming the person you would like to be, start writing them down.

Keep this list handy. At the end of a week or so, examine your list and pull out one particular block that is standing in your way of doing something you would like to do now.

An example of this could be fear of a job interview. Let us say, for example, that you have an appointment next week. Every time you think about this event your stomach turns, your hands begin to get sweaty and your mind goes blank. You try to think about what you are going to say and nothing comes.

Most likely old images from other times come into your mind, other times when you have had poor interviews. Or times when old tapes played telling you you weren't as good as other people. How about the time that you were called on in school and you forgot all the answers and felt foolish in front of the entire class. These were the tapes that you got in touch with as you listened to your *self-talk*.

Now get yourself into a relaxed state. Bring up your relaxation symbol. Gradually begin to quiet your mind and begin to picture yourself getting ready for a very successful interview. Picture yourself dressed very appropriately so that you feel very good about yourself. Take a look in the mirror of your mind and know that you look terrific.

Now let yourself be filled with powerful, positive feelings.

FEEL yourself confident.

FILL yourself with confidence and good feelings.

KNOW you are perfect for this job.

KNOW that there is not a better person for this job.

Now let yourself see yourself going through all the scenes of the interview. Picture yourself sitting down in a chair in the office. See the person who is interviewing you sitting in a chair across from you. Know that no matter what this person looks like, there is real concern and caring about you and your ability to do the job. Carry on an imaginary conversation. When you are through, thank this person very much and leave the office.

Absolutely *know* that if this job is right for you, you will get it. If it is not, the right job is going to appear very quickly.

Let yourself feel the good feelings of having had a successful interview. Let yourself know that you have done a good job.

Congratulate yourself!

After doing this visualization for a few days, your thoughts will begin to change about the upcoming interview and you actually will begin to feel more relaxed and confident about it. By the time that the interview really takes place, you will be able to walk in as if you have been there before and will not experience the panic that you might have in a brand new situation.

Visualizations work because the mind gives the body positive messages. Your body begins to get used to experiencing new ways to feel. New tapes are created and new buttons are pushed.

Whenever you are doing something new, learn to visualize it first in a positive way. Always see yourself as the person you would like to be, acting in a way that you would like to act. *Never* allow old visions to come in from the past.

Once you are able to VISUALIZE the new you . . . You need to AFFIRM the new you. First SEE IT . . . and then SAY IT. SAY IT over and over and over again . . . And in time the new tape will be playing automatically!

Your Affirmation

"Today I picture myself flooded in the glow of a powerful, bright light that is guiding me on my positive path of success and happiness."

31

Affirmations

*"We become what we want to be by believing
and affirming that we already are . . ."*

A Course of Miracles

Affirmations are wonderful tools to help us turn around negative thoughts and habits into positive ones. They help us put positive energy into our lives and release the blocks that are holding us back.

The dictionary states that to affirm is to state positively or with confidence; declare to be true. An affirmation is asserting that a fact is so.

**If we believe that we are going to change . . .
we are going to change!**

An affirmation is a positive thought that we imagine as if it were true in the now. If we say it and feel it with conviction, it will become true. An affirmation is written or stated positively.

"[Affirmation] is an act of courage on the spiritual level, for it is a positive thought form in the face of an unknown situation."

Ruth Ross,
The Prosperous Woman

Affirming is not the same as wishing and is far more powerful. Affirming states that something is so. It *makes firm* a statement or a thought. Wishing is a 'maybe it will and maybe it won't.'

Shakti Gawain in *Creative Visualization* adds that affirmations should always be stated in the most positive way possible. They should be short and simple, a clear statement conveying a strong meaning. Affirmations should always feel totally right for you. You are not trying to redo something from the past but to create something brand new. They should create a feeling of belief. You should say them with conviction. Affirmations acknowledge the Universal source of all things.

Affirmations are positive statements we say to ourselves. They need to have four qualities to be successful:

1. Conviction

If we say them with conviction, we begin the process of internalizing the positive statements that we tell ourselves. If we feel what we tell ourselves is true in the present, our affirmation does become true in the present.

If you really do not believe what you are affirming, and you sincerely want it to be true, then give it "lip service". Act as if you believe it. If you "act as if" enough times, you will come to believe it to be true.

As you say it with conviction you are *energizing* your affirmation. Let yourself *feel* your affirmation by actually visualizing it as real in the now. Let the good *feelings* pour through your body as you begin to reprogram yourself.

2. Present Tense

We state them as if they are happening and real now. We do not say this *will* happen, because that is denying its existence in the now. **By telling ourselves it is now real, it will become real** in our subconscious. The subconscious does not know if something is happening in reality or only in the mind. It registers feelings and emotions. Therefore, if it is real in the mind, it is real in the subconscious.

3. Energy

Affirmations must be said with positive feelings and with energy. They have to be stated so that they are felt with your body. For example, if you are affirming that you feel good about yourself, imagine how your body would feel if you felt good and became aware of those bodily feelings.

4. Repetition

Affirmations must be repeated either orally or in writing for them to become part of us. Experiments have proven that we can change in 21 days if we repeat our affirmation at least 10 times each day.

To state something positive about ourselves is probably a very unfamiliar point of view for many of us who have been so used to thinking of ourselves in a negative fashion.

Very often we automatically react to anything good we want to do or think we want to be by saying "I can't," or "I don't deserve." And then we give ourselves a lot of stories and rationalizations to make "I can't" seem real. These negative tapes (thoughts) are the BLOCKS that keep us from finding our true selves, from finding the good within us.

These are old tapes from yesterday. This is how we let our yesterdays control our todays and this is why things do not change and get better.

By giving up alcohol, drugs and other dependencies, we have made a very powerful positive statement. We have removed the biggest BLOCK we had! We made extraordinary, miraculous progress! We have probably acted on the first bit of faith in positives in a long time.

Things surely don't feel better when we withdraw and deprive ourselves of something we so desperately want. But we begin to believe that if we stay away from these substitutes for long enough, our lives will get better. Now in abstinence we get in touch with the insanity of our minds, especially when our minds tell us that just one drink or drug or sweet or whatever will make us feel better.

And the longer that we stay away from our addictions, add a recovery program to our lives and then begin to meditate, the more we begin to hear all the other negative and destructive tapes that continue to keep us in places that are not good for us and keep us filled with feelings that we do not want to have.

The important things to remember about affirmations are that:

1. *They are stated in the present tense, in the NOW.*
2. *They are positive.*
3. *You act and feel as if they are true.*
4. *You feel good about what you are saying.*
5. *You repeat them at least 10 times a day for 21 days.*

It Is Time To Get Unblocked!

It is time to be rid of those blocks that have kept us imprisoned in our past for so long.

Here are a few examples of affirmations:

I am discovering with joy who I am!

Today I feel the power and the energy of the universe at my fingertips.

I am moving through this day easily and effortlessly.

I deserve wonderful things to happen to me.

I am finding a life for me that is perfect for who I am.

*I have all the time that I need to do all that is good
and right in my life.*

☆

I am a lovable and loving person.

☆

My Higher Power is always with me and guiding me.

☆

*I am connected with the positive and loving energies
of the universe.*

☆

I feel peace and love not anger and guilt.

☆

My past no longer owns me.

☆

I am free of old, negative feelings.

☆

I forgive myself and all others today.

☆

I am one with my Higher Power and the Universe today.

☆

*I no longer give power to the conversations that go on
in my head.*

☆

Dr. Joseph Murphy in his book, *The Power of Your Subconscious*, has a wonderful affirmation for healing:

"My body and all its organs were created by a Higher Power. It knows how to heal me. Its wisdom fashioned all my organs, tissues, muscles and bones. The infinite healing presence within me is now transforming every atom of my being making me whole and perfect now.

"I give thanks for the healing I know is taking place now. Wonderful are the works of a Power greater than myself, the God or Creative Intelligence within me."

Now Write Your Own Affirmations

Pick one area of your life that you feel has had a negative effect on your growth. Listen to your SELF-TALK. Hear what you tell yourself when you think that something is difficult. Listen to the messages that your mind gives you over and over again.

Make a commitment to a *new* program of positive change!

First, meditate at least 10 minutes to quiet your mind. Then you can hear and clear your mind to become open to positive change.

Second, visualize the new change you want to make. Visualize yourself as if the change has already taken place. Put energy and feelings into your visualization and believe it to be true. Remember to give lip service, to "act as if" if at first you don't believe it. This is not a lie that you are telling yourself. It is a reprocessing of old tapes at your subconscious level.

Let yourself **FEEL** as if the thought were true. Put energy into how you would feel if this were real in the now. Visualize yourself as new with all your new feelings.

Write your affirmations at least 10 times, saying them with conviction and energy and do this for 21 days.

Know that God is giving you all the energy you need to make this or something better for you a reality in your life today.

Your Affirmations:

_____

_____

_____

_____

_____

32

Gentle Meditation For Gentle People

"Meditation is the spiritual way to turn my thoughts away from whatever is troubling me. It is a lift, a refreshment."

One Day at a Time in Al-Anon

You can pick a meditation at random or you can just read one after another until you find that feeling that you would like to feel, until you get to that special place within where you would like to be.

The following pages consist of simple meditations to help you to relax, sleep, relieve anxiety or stress. They can help you to feel better about yourself or a situation that is bothering you, or perhaps just to slow down so you can enjoy the moment. You can read them very slowly to yourself or have them read slowly by someone else.

If while doing them you find yourself experiencing anxiety or frustration, know that it is perfectly normal. Don't waste energy putting yourself down or judging yourself. Stay with whatever you are feeling. Remember that the first reactions that usually come up are urges either to run or to hide from stress. We want to feel better immediately. However, we can choose instead to take this as an opportunity to expand our comfort zone by learning that we do not have to run or hide. You will see that if you just stay with the feelings, you will discover that they are not permanent, that they will pass if you just accept them.

There is no fault to be placed here. Whatever you are feeling is OK. Whatever you are feeling is just whatever you are feeling. It is perfect!

It is perfect because you are now going to see that you do not have to keep these feelings. You do not have to let these feelings take you over. You do not have to hold on to these feelings. And most important, without running away or giving in to any addiction . . . you can change these feelings *now*, and eventually forever.

> In either case . . .
> . . . breathe deeply . . . and slowly . . . while
> you are reading or hearing them . . .
> Take time to let the words
>   sink
>   in
>   with
>   each
>   breath.
> Hear the gentleness of the words . . .
>   Feel the softness of the words . . .
>   as you let the feeling of
>   *love*
>   come
>   in.
> Breathe in and
>   breathe out . . .

Chances are that you picked up this book because you are stressed or concerned about something. Let yourself know that this is all right. There does not have to be something wrong with you just because you are feeling this way. Usually until we know better, most of us immediately begin to beat ourselves with the stick of self-pity and remorse, taking on the heavy burden of blame and guilt for our feelings.

Know that there is no fault here. Whatever you are feeling is OK! Whatever you are feeling is just whatever you are feeling. It is perfect!

It is perfect because you are now going to see that you do not have to keep these feelings. You do not have to let these feelings take you over. You do not have to hold on to these feelings. And, most important, without any psychoanalysis, deep insight, running away or giving in to any addiction . . . you can change these feelings *now* and, eventually forever!!!

Always begin with the *Basic Meditation*.

Always begin by bringing attention to your breath . . . slowly and gently . . . while you are reading and listening to the words.

Take a few moments to get comfortable.

Make sure your clothing is loose and not binding.

Bring your attention to your breath
    as you breathe in
        and as you breathe out . . .
    As you breathe in
        and as you breathe out.
Take time to let the words
    sink
      in
        with
          each
            breath.
Hear the gentleness of the words . . .
    Feel the softness of the words . . .
        as you let the feeling of
        love
          come
            in.
    Breathe in and
        breathe out . . .

Meditation While Walking

Try this simple walking meditation for just five minutes and see how relaxed it can make you feel. This can be most useful if you are at one of those stressful times when all you can think about is release and escape in a drink or a drug . . . or food . . . or in any addiction or other escape. Pray to live instead and be gentle with yourself. Your mind and your body might be screaming for relief. But there are other ways to relieve stress and *you are at choice.* Here is one choice that will help you to be good to yourself!

This is, of course, just as useful if you are uptight or nervous. It is relaxing and refreshing and helps you feel alive and in charge of your life and your moods!

Take a few minutes to get in touch with your breath as you begin to breathe in and breathe out with awareness.

Begin to walk very slowly.

Begin to bring attention to your feet as they touch the ground.

Begin to feel what is happening as each part of your foot meets with the ground.

Bring attention to your arms as they swing by your side.

Bring attention to your head and then to the back of your neck.

Now let your attention go from your head to your neck and throughout your body, finding any areas that are tight and uncomfortable.

Keep your attention on those areas and let relaxation flow through them.

Notice the movement of your body as everything moves while you are walking.

Now bring attention to your breath as it goes in and out as you are walking.

And if thoughts come in, as they will, just gently notice them and bring your attention back to your walking. Go back and bring attention to your feet as they touch the ground, and your arms as they swing by your sides and your head as it sits on the top of your neck which sits on the top of your shoulders.

Feel the Difference . . .
    as you become aware of the now . . .
        know the difference . . .
          Enjoy the difference!

Just Take Five Minutes To Feel Good About Yourselves

This is a wonderful exercise to do with a partner. Take turns reading this to each other. You will be amazed how good you can feel to be the reader, knowing that you are helping someone else feel as good as you would like to feel.

Speak softly and with as much love as you can, knowing that it will be returned to you soon. You will see, too, that as you give, you receive, that love given away is never lost!

You are going to begin very gently to change the negative attitudes you have about yourself. You didn't become an addict because you felt good about yourself. You didn't abuse alcohol or drugs because you felt good when you were clean and sober. You didn't drink destructively because you thought you were a special, lovable person.

Relax and begin to breathe in and out very slowly.

Begin to think of yourself as a kind and loving person. If this is hard, or you think it silly, please do it anyway. Know that you deserve good and wonderful things in life!

Know you are special and you are on earth to do very special things with your life.

If a negative thought comes in, refuse to accept it. *Be in Charge.* Bring your attention back to your breathing if the thought won't go away.

This is your time to feel
 Good
  and
   Soft
    and
     Lovable.

Close your eyes and allow yourself to feel your goodness. Feel your gentleness. Feel loved and secure and alive and healthy.

If you do this for only five minutes every day, you will begin to feel it more and more the rest of your day. And you will begin to accept it as true . . .

BECAUSE
 IT
  IS!

When You Really Want To Escape With A Drink Or A Drug . . .

Try something spiritual instead of spirits!

Meditation can be very useful when you are having a difficult time not drinking or drugging!

Just two ingredients are needed. One is a desire to have a desire to quit. It is not even necessary to have a sincere desire yet. And the second is that you are in touch with a power greater than your self, or that you are willing to give lip service to a power greater than yourself, whether you believe in one or not. This power can be God, a Universal

Force, Allah, Buddha or any other power that is greater than you and is a power for good and love in the universe. If you can say *yes* to just these two elements, you are halfway there.

There are a number of exercises in this book that will help you to relax. They all help to relieve tensions that build up quite naturally when you are giving up and letting go of an addiction. All difficult situations which used to be eased by picking up a drink or drug now make our bodies scream out loud for relief. It would also be helpful to read the exercise for *feeling good* about yourself when you feel like escaping into your addiction.

Discover Your Source Of Power

Once you know that you are powerless over your addiction, you then will discover that you are at **choice.**

You will see now that if you *choose* to *stop* you have all the energy that you need to accomplish what you set out to do.

Please begin by making yourself very comfortable. Make sure your clothing is loose enough so that it won't bind you. Find a quiet place where you won't be disturbed. Relax. (Refer to section on *How To Meditate* if you need to.) If at all possible, have someone read this aloud to you.

Now just close your eyes and breathe very deeply in and out through your nose very slowly ten times.

Relax . . .

Know that you deserve to be good and gentle with yourself. You deserve all good things. You deserve all that you want that is good for you. You, above all, deserve to love yourself. You will. You have all that you need to be good to yourself. You have all that you need to be happy. You will learn to get in touch with that force that gives you the energies for love and happiness and health.

Close your eyes and let yourself *feel* that strength coming in to you with every breath.

Every time you breathe in, you are taking in *powerful* energies for good and love.

Every time you breathe out, you are forcing out poisons and dirt that have blocked you from the light and power of health and love.

Know that every time you breathe in, you are being filled with all the power that you need for the moment.

Breathe in positive energy.

Breathe out darkness and negativity.

Breathe in powerful forces for positive good.

Breathe out all that is negative
   and keeping you from seeing
     the light.

Breathe in . . . breathe out
   in . . . out.
     You are becoming cleansed.
      You are becoming healed.
       You are not Drinking or Drugging!
        Give Thanks!!!

Visualization For Goals

We are going to do this visualization
   easily
     and effortlessly.

There is no need to struggle.

Know that you are open
   to all the positive powers
     of the universe.

Know that you deserve to have
   all the abundance
     the universe has to offer.

There is no struggle involved here.

Just visualize and
  feel the flow of energy
    as it is happening right now in your life.

Let go of all the struggle and tension.

Let go of all the *trying*
  and *struggle*
    and *working hard at it.*

Just picture your goal easily and effortlessly.

Relax and let it happen . . . first in your mind and
  then in your physical world . . . your reality.

Feel how good it feels
  to have what is good
    and right for you.

Feel how good it feels
  to know you are worthy
    to have a full and abundant life.

" *i visualize myself as if this has
          already occurred!* "

Feel the good feelings.

Know that you deserve them.

Smile as you let yourself enjoy
seeing your goal
and feeling your goal.

Know that these positive forces are active in your life at
all times. You can always enjoy them as long as you are willing
and open.

PURPLE VELVET*
A Visualization For Healing

(Both Spiritually and Physically)

This is a beautiful exercise to use when you want to relax
and unwind. It is great if you are feeling uptight, and it is
especially good if negative, self-destructive thoughts begin to
come to your mind. Thoughts like . . .

"I never do anything right!"

or

"I know they won't think I'm good enough!"

or

"No one will know if I smoke a joint!"

or

"One candy bar won't hurt!"

. . . I could go on and on, but . . .

You have the picture!

---

*If another color seems more soothing or healing or spiritual for you, simply substitute
your color for purple.

Place yourself in a comfortable, meditative position. Close your eyes and spend a few minutes becoming aware of your breathing.

Slowly take a few minutes to
   begin to
    feel
      your breath
As it goes in and
  as it comes out.
Begin to let yourself
  Feel
    the power of your breath
      as it enters your body.
Feel
  the power of your breath
    as it goes in.
Feel
  the softness of your breath
    as it goes out.

When you feel a bit more calmed down and have more of a sense of well being, begin to bring your attention to the parts of your body that feel uptight or in pain. Let your attention stay with that area.

Now, let your mind see a soft beautiful piece of velvet. If you can't see it, that's OK, too. Just let yourself feel what it might be like. See it or feel it. Or both.

Let that *soft* velvet float before you. Let it float within you. Now let it float to where you are uptight or in pain.

Let it go in and let it go out of your pain. Let it go in and let it go out of your stress. Let it go in and let it go out of the muscles and the tendons and the skin and the bones that are all surrounding the area of your discomfort.

Let it float and caress your body.

Know that every time you are breathing in, you are breathing in healing power. Know that you are breathing in positive energy for good and for love.

Let yourself know that you deserve to feel beautiful and lovely and soft and to be caressed.

Let the purple velvet float and caress and soothe your anxiety and your stress and your tension and your pain.

Let it smooth out
   all the rough places
      in your mind and your body
         and let it bring you
            peace.

Now bring your attention to the air that surrounds your body.

Know that the air that surrounds your body has all the same qualities as your piece of velvet.

Know that when you open your eyes, the air that surrounds your body will continue to caress and heal you.

The air that surrounds your body will smooth over
   all the rough and sore and tired places
      in your mind and your body
         and gently
           bring you
            peace.

"... watch for miracles!"

The Story Of The God Bag

In 1976 Sandra Bierig, my partner, and I started Serenity House, a recovery home for alcoholic women in Natick, Massachusetts. We barely had enough money for food on the table, let alone enough to pay our bills. We were constantly worrying, hardly sleeping at night, wondering where the next meal was going to come from. The strain was really beginning to show when one day a dear friend, Jane, shared a story with us.

She told us the story of a little old lady in California who was very often in trouble. It seemed that every time she tried to do something her way, it would really turn out badly. But she had a God Bag. And the times that she remembered to write down some problem or other and turn it over to her Higher Power by putting it in the God Bag, everything would work out just fine.

Often the little old lady would put a problem in the God Bag, but then she would get impatient while waiting for results. She would try to handle it herself, until she saw it going badly again and would put it back in the God Bag again mentally. Lo and behold, the problem always worked out just fine when she did that.

Well, if it worked for a little old lady in California, just maybe it would work for us. So Barbara, one of our first residents, stitched a simple God Bag for us out of some green burlap. (We still have it today.) And we all rushed to write down everything that was worrying us.

Miracles did start happening. Donations started to come in. The Division of Alcoholism gave us our first contract. (We have had one with them ever since.) Food seemed to appear from nowhere and donations of beds and bureaus began to arrive at our front door. But the biggest miracle of all was that women started to get sober! And that was, after all, the purpose of it all.

Just like the little old lady from California, every time we became impatient and took our problems back, the worry would return and things started going badly. But when we let them go, things just seemed to work out miraculously.

God Bags work! Thank God!

God Bag Visualization

As you begin all visualizations, find a comfortable, quiet place and relax. Sit quietly and close your eyes and breathe in and breathe out very slowly. Take a few minutes to notice your breath as you breathe in and you breathe out. Bring your attention to your breath as you breathe in and you breathe out.

Relax all parts of your body, bringing attention to any part that might feel strain or anxiety.

And picture in your mind the most beautiful God Bag for yourself . . .

Any color that you like . . .

Any material that you like.

Create your very own God Bag in your mind,
decorating it in
your own special way . . .
either with paints . . .
or with materials . . .
or with stitching.

Or anything else that you can think of to make it your very own.

Know that this is a very special bag, a miraculous bag!

You don't even have to call it a God Bag if you'd rather not. It can be your Higher Power bag or a Positive Energy Bag or whatever you choose.

You can bring up your imaginary God Bag anytime and anywhere. It is always with you! Know that you have created something that can always work for you, whenever you remember it is there.

Now, in your mind get a pencil and paper. Sit very quietly and write down everything that might come up for you that is concerning you right now . . . all your anxieties . . . anyone that you might be concerned about, your family or your friends. Think of any problems that you might have and write them down.

Now fold the paper very gently. Are you sure that you covered everything? Add anything else that might come up, anything that you have not been able to handle.

Fold your paper again and put it in your God Bag. Notice that the God Bag has been designed with two sturdy handles at the top.

Now picture a very large, beautiful balloon. It can be any color that you want it to be. Picture this large balloon over your head . . . up in the sky.

It is a beautiful day and this magnificent balloon is just hanging there above you . . . floating gently above your head . . . just floating . . . waiting for you.

Notice that there is a string hanging from your balloon. The string is tied to the balloon just waiting for you to hold it. See the string just floating there . . . waiting for you to take it in your hand.

Reach up and take the string. Now tie it to the handles of your God Bag. Tie it nice and tight. Now watch the balloon as it floats higher and higher up into the universe. See it floating higher and higher into the sky . . . above the clouds . . .

Watch it become smaller and smaller as it floats higher and higher . . . carrying your God Bag up into the heavens, up into the Powers of the Universe, up into the Powers of your Higher Power . . . God.

Now that it is carrying everything that you have written in your God Bag . . . all your problems . . . all your negative feelings . . . all that you want to turn over to your Higher Power . . . everything that you cannot handle alone.

Know that your balloon is carrying your God Bag up to the powers of the universe and you have done everything that you can do right now that is good and right in your life.

Now feel a tremendous relief as all the weight that you have been carrying on your shoulders is removed as it floats higher and higher to your Higher Power in your God Bag.

All your fears are being removed as you feel lighter and lighter, knowing that everything is right in the Universe . . . that order and balance is returning to your life as you feel lighter and lighter.

Know that you are free as "God is doing for you what you could not do for yourself."

Now very slowly come back to your room. Be sure you count to five before you open your eyes.

It is really very helpful to make a real physical God Bag, too. You can take just a paper bag if you like. Actually take a piece of paper, write down what you cannot handle, put it in the God Bag and watch for miracles!

Your Affirmation

"God is giving me all the energy that I need to make positive changes in my life today!"

letting go feels good!!

33

Becoming The Best
Of Who We Are

*"Who really knows the effect of one happy thought?
Is it possible that it circles the globe, finding entry
into any open heart, encouraging and giving hope
in some unseen way? I am convinced it does. For
whenever I am truly loving, I feel the warmth and
presence of the like-minded, a growing family whose
strength lies in their gentleness and whose message
is in their treatment of others."*

Hugh Prather

We have traveled a long road together and have come
to many new places. You have acquired many new tools along
the way. These tools can be used at any time.

Remember, you can be the best of who you are by taking
full responsibility for your life. You never have to be a victim
to anyone or anything again. When you know that you are
at cause, when you know that you deserve to be happy and
fulfilled, then your life will just get better.

You are in charge of you now! This puts *you* in charge
of your future!

After meditating for many days to better understand human suffering, the Buddha was asked what he had learned.

"I am awake," he answered.

Be awake! Be alive! Be in charge! May your journey be filled with joy and light and love and peace. Know that the power of the universe is always with you, that a power greater than yourself is only as far as a breath away. And may you share your knowledge and your love with all who join you on your Spiritual Path to Recovery.

Thank you for joining me on mine.

Recommended Reading List

Adult Children of Alcoholics, Janet Woititz, Health Communications, Pompano Beach, Florida, 1983. *New York Times* best seller on subject.

Affirmations — 21 Day Workshop, Ruth Fishel. A 21-day program designed for your personal use.*

Anatomy of an Illness: As Perceived by the Patient, Norman Cousins. W.W. Norton and Co., Inc., Bantam Edition, 1981. Excellent true story of positive thinking in in healing disease.

The Aquarian Conspiracy, Marilyn Ferguson. Moving and inspiring book on the Human Potential and Spiritual Movement in the world today.

A Course of Miracles. Three-volume course centering on the need for forgiveness for healing. Extraordinarily inspirational and enlightening.*

Children of Alcoholics, Robert Ackerman. Learning Publications, Holmes Beach, Florida, 1978. Good information for children and adult children of alcoholics.

Choicemaking, Sharon Wegscheider-Cruse. Health Communications, Pompano Beach, Florida, 1985. Good information for co-dependents and adult children of alcoholics.

Creative Visualization, Ronald Shone. Thorsons Publishers, Inc., 377 Park Ave. South, New York, NY 10016, 1984.

Creative Visualization, Shakti Gawain. Whatever Publishing, Inc., 1979; Bantam Books Inc., 1982. Clear and easy-to-follow techniques for relaxation, opening energy centers, affirmations, creating and following through with goals, etc.*

Each Day A New Beginning. The Hazelden Foundation, Box 176, Center City, MN 55012, 1982. A wonderful way for women to begin their day. A daily book of inspirational meditations for women in recovery.*

Emmanuel's Book compiled by Pat Rodegast and Judith Stanton. Friends Press, P.O. Box 1006, Weston, CT, 1985. A delightful book full of wisdom on a variety of subjects. A manual for living comfortably in the cosmos.

From Medication to Meditation, Ruth Fishel, Positives Unlimited, 1985. Gentle introduction to meditation as a useful tool in recovery of addictions.*

Getting Well Again, O. Carl Simonton, Stephanie Mathews-Simonton and James L. Creighton. Bantam Books, Inc., New York, 1978. Highly successful program of healing in cancer which can be adapted for any other illness.

God Makes The Rivers To Flow. Passages for meditation selected by Eknath Easwaran. Nilgiri Press, 1982. An inspiring collection of meditations from all major religions throughout the ages.*

A Gradual Awakening, Steven Levine. Anchor Books, Anchor Press/Doubleday, Garden City, New York, 1979. Gentle and beautifully moving guide to Insight Meditation.

How Can I Help? Ram Dass and Paul Gorman. Alfred A. Knopf, New York, 1985. This should be a must for everyone in the helping professions and those who are moved to help others in their daily life. Excellent sections on dealing with and avoiding burnout.

Journey of Awakening: A Meditator's Guidebook, Ram Dass. Bantam Books, New York, 1985.

Living in the Light, Shakti Gawain. Whatever Publishing Company, P.O. Box 137, Mill Valley, CA 94942, 1986. Clear, practical guide to learn to trust your intuition and develop creativity.

Love Is Letting Go Of Fear, Gerald G. Jampolsky. Bantam Books, 1981. The founder of the Center for Attitudinal Healing offers simple advice for spiritual growth based on A Course in Miracles.*

The Llewellyn Practical Guide To Creative Visualization. Melita Denning and Osborne Phillips, 1980. Llewellyn Publications, Inc.

Meditation, An Eight-point Program, Eknath Easwaran. Blue Mountain Center of Meditation, 1978. Obtained from Nilgiri Press, Box 477, Petaluma, CA 94953. Inspirational. A good place to begin in the morning.*

The Miracle of Mindfulness! Thich Nhat Hanh. Beacon Press, Boston, MA, 1976. A simple, gentle book that teaches Mahayana and Theravada traditions of Buddhist meditation.

Mother Wit, Diane Mariechild. The Crossing Press, Trumansburg, New York, 1981.

The Myth of Freedom and **The Way of Meditation** by Chogyam Trungpa, Shambhala Publications, Boulder, CO, 1976.

Open Mind, Open Heart, Thomas Keating. Amity House, 106 Newport Bridge Rd., Warwick, N.Y., 1986. Christian-based meditation with step-by-step guidance in centering prayer.

Prospering Woman, Ruth Ross. Whatever Publishing, Inc., 1982. Helps us to discover the negative blocks that keep us from prospering. Use of affirmations and visualizations to turn them around.*

Shame and Guilt: Characteristics of the Dependency Cycle. Ernest Kurtz. Hazelden Foundation, 1984.

Tantra For The West—A Guide To Personal Freedom, Marcus Allen. Whatever Publishing, 1978. Techniques in all areas including health, food, money, sex., etc. Easy to follow and understand.

Teach Only Love, Gerald G. Jampolsky. Bantam, 1983. See description of **Love Is Letting Go Of Fear.***

Twelve Steps and Twelve Traditions. Alcoholics Anonymous World Services, Inc., Box 459, Grand Central Station, New York, NY 10163, 1952. A must for anyone in a recovery program. The basic program for growth and recovery for all programs based on the principles of AA.*

Twenty Four Hours A Day. Hazelden Foundation, Center City, MN 55012, 1954. Especially for recovering alcoholics. A daily meditation book to help begin each day in recovery.*

Woman Spirit, Hallie Iglehart. Harper and Row Publishers, San Francisco, 1983.

Working Inside Out, Margo Adair. Wingbow Press, Distributed by People Books, Berkeley, CA 94710, 1984.

The Way Of Zen, Alan W. Watts. Pantheon Books, Inc. 1957.

Zen In The Art Of Archery, Eugene Herrigel. Pantheon Books, Inc., 1953. Vintage Books Edition, 1971.

*Books starred are carried at Serenity Inc., 11 Pond Street, Natick, MA 01760